CRACK

Treating Cocaine Addiction

George
Medzerian, Ph.D.

 Human Services Institute
Bradenton, Florida

 **TAB BOOKS**
Blue Ridge Summit, PA

Human Services Institute publishes books on human problems, especially those affecting families and relationships: addiction, stress, alienation, violence, parenting, gender, and health. Experts in psychology, medicine, and the social sciences have gained invaluable new knowledge about prevention and treatment, but there is a need to make this information available to the public. Human Services Institute books help bridge the information gap between experts and people with problems.

FIRST EDITION
SECOND PRINTING

© 1991 by **HSI/TAB Books**.
TAB Books is a division of McGraw-Hill, Inc.

Library of Congress Cataloging-in-Publication Data

Medzerian, George.
    Crack : treating cocaine addiction / by George Medzerian.
      p.   cm.
    Includes index.
    ISBN 0-8306-3622-6 (pbk.)
    1. Crack (Drug) 2. Cocaine habit—Treatment. 3. Narcotic addicts—Counseling of. I. Title.
    [DNLM: 1. Cocaine. 2. Counseling. 3. Substance Dependence. WM 280 M493c]
    RC568.C6M43   1991
    616.86'470651—dc20
    DNLM/DLC
    for Library of Congress   91-534
                                                  CIP

TAB Books offers software for sale. For information and a catalog, please contact TAB Software Department, Blue Ridge Summit, PA 17294-0850.

The publication of this material does not imply affiliation with nor approval or endorsement from Alcoholics Anonymous World Services, Inc., Narcotics Anonymous World Services, Inc. or any other Twelve-Step Fellowship.

Acquisitions Editor: Kimberly Tabor
Development Editor: Lee Marvin Joiner, Ph.D.
Copy Editor: Pat Holliday
Cover Design: Lori E. Schlosser
Cover Photograph: Susan Riley, Harrisonburg, VA

Questions regarding the content of this book should be addressed to:

Human Services Institute, Inc.
P.O. Box 14610
Bradenton, FL 34280

To my wife Barbara for all her support, and to my friends, professional colleagues, and the thousands of addicts who have touched my life. You know who you are . . . Thanks!

Contents

Preface

This book contains a collection of ideas and concepts about treating addiction to crack cocaine based on my experience with addicts and the professionals who work with them every day. It offers new insights into what is termed the *Disease of Addiction*.

Most counselors have difficulty working with crack addicts. Their problems are not the result of a knowledge gap in technical counseling skills. There are good classes, books, and teachers from which to learn established and validated counseling techniques. Although it is always desirable for counselors to improve their technical skills, doing so may not dramatically improve their results with crack addicts. Armed only with refined technical skills, counselors would be like ace auto mechanics driving from New York to Los Angeles without the right map. Although they could fix a car's mechanical problems, they might never reach L.A. In the chemical dependency field we have maps——beliefs about how addicts think, function, and become addicted——but I believe these maps often are the wrong ones for treating addiction to crack cocaine.

Doubt——you may have experienced it in your work with crack addicts; occasions when the techniques you have been taught to use don't seem to work and the answers you have been taught to believe seem wrong . . . that feeling of juggling jelly. It can happen in individual counseling, in group therapy or in informal bull sessions with peers. Doubt, even if just a whisper, can be disturbing because it challenges what we "ought" to believe about addiction or chemical dependency treatment.

If we are counselors recovering from chemical dependency, we feel guilty for questioning the logic behind our own treatment. After all, it saved our lives. During a break at a workshop at the Southeastern School on Addiction Studies a fellow chemical dependency counselor was sitting across the table from me in the lounge area. "Are you a presenter?" he asked. I replied that I was a psychologist presenting a workshop on confrontation in therapeutic communities. He then asked if I believed that the Twelve-Step Fellowship was the best treatment method for all addicts——alcoholics, opiate addicts, and crack addicts. I told him that while I believed strongly in the value of Twelve-Step programs, research shows that for every 100 people who choose AA or NA as their method of continuing care and sobriety, only 26 are still involved in these programs one year later. I went on to say that drug counselors need to do one of two things: either motivate the 74 percent who drop out of Twelve-Step programs to continue, or offer other aftercare and continuing-care programs for people who just can't accept the Twelve Steps. To this he responded, "Well, I never liked you psychologist types. You're only in this for the money. As for me, I'm a recovering addict and I would rather see a chemically dependent person die than offer him anything other than a Twelve-Step program. It's the best." Saved by this program, to question it was to question his entire recovery.

Nonrecovering counselors bite their tongues rather than admit to their peers that they see crack addiction as unresponsive to conventional treatment. In a workshop I offer to counselors-in-training, participants lead group sessions and have their leadership styles critiqued. Often significant personal issues arise when counselors receive training in group skills. A recurring issue expressed by nonrecovering counselors was that they felt excluded, not fully accepted by other chemical dependency counselors because of their lack of a history of addiction. Often these nonrecovering counselors-in-training reacted by saying things like, "I'm not recovering from chemical dependency, but I'm like you because I'm an adult child from an alcoholic family." Or, "I'm not recovering, but I came from a high-stress family so I am kinda like you . . . I can relate." Or, "I'm not a recovering addict, but I know a lot of people who are, and they think I'm okay." The result of this perceived peer pressure is a tendency to go along with a don't-challenge-our-methods mentality.

At a recent professional development conference for addiction counselors, a speaker presented his unorthodox ideas about drug addiction. Many conference participants harbored strong resentments for the remaining week of the conference because the speaker, the instructor from whom they came to learn more about addictions, didn't reinforce their existing professional beliefs. Instead, he challenged their thinking. These social-professional dynamics keep chemical dependency counselors in a mindset that can inhibit them from considering new ideas that could, in turn, lead to higher success rates in treatment.

Chemical dependency counselors often tell their crack addicted clients that it isn't necessary for them to know why they became addicted. This knowledge will not halt their addiction. The counselor, on the other hand, tries to see clearly into the addict's intimate and personal world. Through education, professional training, and clinical experience, counselors develop firm ideas about how addicts think and behave. We explain how people become addicted, why they maintain their addictive patterns, and why they recover or relapse after primary treatment. But what about us? How did we come to view addiction as we do? Answering this question is fundamental to creating an effective treatment approach to crack addiction.

I have divided this book into two parts. *Part One* examines several basic issues surrounding our widely-accepted beliefs, our training and practices as addiction counselors. It presents a new way to view our profession. In chemical dependency counseling we speak of the client's need for faith, but this applies equally to counselors. As counselors we must have enough faith in ourselves to reach out to the new. I believe that the materials and concepts covered in *Part One* are essential for us to consider before unloading our arsenal of clinical skills on crack addicted clients. *Part Two* is the how-to portion. It presents the core skills and essential insights needed to counsel crack addicts effectively, particularly the youthful addicts we encounter so often today. Its nuts-and-bolts approach will generalize to other substance dependencies. *Part Two* provides insights into the special, and sometimes challenging, characteristics and behaviors of crack addicts. These must be understood by any counselor who is considering working with this population. In *Part Two* I also offer some recommendations concerning how to become more effective in the role of chemical dependency counselor.

Before reading this book, I would like you to rate yourself as a counselor on a scale from one to ten. A rating of "one" represents a "brand new" counselor, and "ten" stands for a "hotshot" counselor, a "counselor's counselor." After you have read this book, reevaluate your rating of your skills. A friend, professional colleague, and dynamite family therapist, Dick Jacobs, did this brief exercise with me before his workshop, and I was confronted with the degree of my competence and, painfully, my limitations.

Acknowledgments

I would like to thank the following people and organizations for their contributions to my professional growth and for many of the ideas that I have attempted to incorporate into this book: Dr. Bill Miller of the University of New Mexico; the member agencies of the Florida Alcohol and Drug Abuse Association; Operation PAR; the Florida School of Addiction Studies; Lakeview Center; and the Institute for Integral Development. I am also grateful to St. Xavier's Center in Kathmandu, Nepal; the Florida Association of Voluntary Agencies for Caribbean Action; the United States Information Agency; and the Salvation Army World Service Organization for granting me the opportunity to witness and study chemical dependency treatment outside the United States.

1

Crack: The Addiction

BIRTH AND REBIRTH

of a Chemical Dependency Counselor

I began my work with addictions as a urine monitor in a street clinic for narcotic addicts. The methadone program had about two hundred clients and a clinical staff of five: one ex-addict (we now call them recovering addicts) and four counselors who had never been addicted to drugs. Because many of us had tried drugs as teenagers, we all believed we knew all there was to know about addictions. Many of us had smoked dope, dropped acid, taken uppers and downers, and even done what we then called "hard" drugs, so we thought we knew it all. In retrospect, I guess our staff knew a lot about drug abuse but not much about addiction.

Most of us were trained, in the street or professionally, in psychological (primarily behavioral) treatment methods. We worked as teams, asking help from each other and receiving it with gratitude. We were hungry to learn. We sought better ways to treat addicts, and invented some impressive treatment modalities. Our need to observe, understand, and discover kept everyone alert, reading and experimenting with new, creative treatment techniques. We made mistakes, but they were the result of our honest attempts to stretch ourselves and our skills. That was good in some ways and, looking back from today, this clinic provided one of my best professional learning experiences.

After six months of watching men urinate in bottles, I was promoted to entry-level counselor. I called myself a therapist though, as all new counselors do. I walked into my first office and before me were ninety-three active and inactive charts. There I was, twenty-three years old, with the responsibility to "fix" approximately ninety-three hard core "dope fiends." I was overwhelmed, but young and naively confident. It dawned on me that I knew nothing of therapy or what I was supposed to do as a therapist.

Chemical dependency counselors, in the early seventies, were not told exactly what to do with addicts. There was no firmly established professional doctrine controlling what we thought or did. Like most students of psychology and the behavioral sciences, I believed my role was to perform therapy based on the exorcism model. By pinpointing the deep-seated, underlying issue that caused the symptom being presented (active drug addiction), I could supposedly resolve the underlying issue and then the addict's symptom and associated problems would disappear. This TV Psychiatrist orientation led me to do some deep, heavy, and flashy "psychotherapy." Counseling was for lightweights. I had become a psychotherapist.

It was amazing to me that after working with a dope fiend for years on an outpatient basis, doing wonderful therapy, I got few good results. The client still shot dope. Even more amazing to me was that helping an addict gain insight didn't seem to change anything. Even after gaining profound insights into their childhood, my clients would still test positive for drug use. I thought my analysis would exorcise the dope from their veins, but when I did my insight therapy with addicts I ended with insightful people who shot dope.

Some addicts stopped using drugs, but they still didn't function well. I remember a client who began treatment with major developmental deficits. He couldn't read or write well. He couldn't balance a checkbook or keep a budget. He stopped using drugs, but still couldn't read or write well, balance a checkbook or keep a budget. He sat in my office, drug-free, combing his hair with a plastic fork.

After about three years of this, I realized that my approach was limited and unreliable. So, I began to read all the books I could find on addiction. The books I read described addicts, told of their plight due to social, environmental, emotional and economic problems. Still, I knew nothing of how to treat addicts successfully.

I began to believe that the chemical dependency itself, the addiction, needed to be put into remission before counseling could work. (By this time I had begun to call what I do "counseling" and not "therapy," because I had so many failures I had learned some humility.) The idea of treating the condition of psychoactive drug use, before dealing with the underlying dynamics or learned behaviors associated with addiction, grew stronger as I studied more psychophysiology and learning theory. I understood that, on a strictly behavioral and physiological basis, shooting dope was so enmeshed with the behaviors, thoughts and feelings of addiction that it would be difficult to separate the act of drug use from its internal and external cues.

I became convinced that an addict who can gain control of the internal and external cues associated with drug use *theoretically* can use psychoactive medications nondestructively. Still, the enmeshment of cues and drug-taking behavior is so strong but subtle, at the unconscious and physiological levels, that this disengagement is extremely rare. The alcohol counselor's concept of total abstinence is effective because by removing the psychoactive substance completely from the addict's experience, the internal cues, the recall of memories, are stopped.

Habits and State-Dependent Learning

Habituation. While studying psychophysiology, I was fascinated with the concepts of habituation and state-dependent learning. Habituation is the basis for systematic desensitization. If someone is exposed repeatedly to the same stimulus, the mind will eventually ignore it. In a psychophysiology laboratory, habituation can be demonstrated with galvanic skin responses and electrocardiograms. I participated in an experiment with the startle reflex. As I sat wired to an electrocardiogram, someone popped balloons behind me at fixed and variable time intervals. The first few pops triggered some major spikes on the electrocardiogram. After several trials, the spikes disappeared. At the physiological level, I had become desensitized or habituated to the popping noise.

Cocaine hydrochloride addicts who inject drugs regularly do not feel the pain of sticking needles into their arms. To a casual observer, it seems inconceivable it is no longer painful. Crack addicts who come home night after night to disappointed, tearful family members, eventually do not feel guilty. The addict becomes desensitized to guilt. The casual observer thinks it's impossible for the crack addict to be that cold or uncaring. He is not cold and uncaring, but desensitized to the guilt by repeated trials. The cocaine whore who barters sex daily for drugs doesn't feel cheapened by performing sex for a piece of rock. Through repetition the crack-addicted prostitute becomes desensitized to the "shame" she felt the first few times. The drug addict shooting dope, the crack addict staggering in the door in front of family members and the cocaine prostitute have normalized their behaviors. They may once have felt the behaviors to be bizarre and perverted. The change was produced by nothing more than systematic desensitization (behavioral) or habituation (physiological).

Systematic desensitization and habituation make people think they are normal even when their behavior appears abnormal to everyone else. This phenomenon relates to what we term "denial." Just because clients fail to see what they are doing as sick, strange, deviant, or abnormal doesn't mean they are in denial. Most behaviors, if repeated enough, assume a quality of normalcy.

State-Dependent Learning. The idea of state-dependent learning is crucial to understanding drug addiction. State-dependent learning means that you recall information best under the same physiological conditions in which it was learned. The implications of this are profound.

Consider the use of methadone maintenance with an opiate addict. In a methadone maintenance program we switch the addict from heroin, Dilaudid or morphine to methadone (cross-tolerance) and maintain the addict on this similar narcotic. This is done for noble reasons. Methadone is purer than street dope, cheaper, legal, and orally ingested. The assumption is that addicts are more stable on a "better" drug. We can treat them, and when they are emotionally, mentally, and socially healthy we can detoxify them into a drug-free, functioning person. Yet when we consider what therapy or counseling is—educating the client and removing resistance—the methadone program makes little sense.

A client is kept on a narcotic, educated (a major part of therapy) and then, as seen from the viewpoint of state-dependent learning, detoxed from the ability to recall what was learned in therapy. Our chances of successful treatment would increase if, instead, we were first to detoxify the addict, move him into the desired physiological (drug free) state, and then "therapize" (educate) him. This approach increases the likelihood that addicts will retain and recall the skills you teach them, which translates into fewer treatment failures. With fewer treatment failures there is less need to blame the client by charging that he is unmotivated, resistant to change, or in denial.

State-dependent memory plays a critical role in relapse and relapse prevention.[1] Often clients who have done superbly in treatment, maintaining abstinence for prolonged periods of time, slip or relapse. The most common reaction of relapsers to a slip is, "I must have gotten nothing from therapy. I have been fooling myself into thinking I was getting better, but I learned nothing. When I used the first time, after six months of sobriety, the old thoughts, feelings and behaviors came back in droves. I guess I'm still sick."

William Schutz stated that people need three elements in life: inclusion, control and affection[2]. Understanding state-dependent learning and its effects in relapse empowers the recovering person with a sense of control over the recovery process. It is reassuring for the relapser to learn that recalling prerecovery thoughts, feelings and behaviors when in the midst of a relapse is normal and due to state-dependent learning. Once clients are aware of this, they are less likely to discount the value of their

---

1. Terence T. Gorski, with CENAPS Corporation, has during the past twenty years written much on relapse prevention. See Terence Gorski and Marlene Miller, *Counseling for Relapse Prevention* (Independence, MO: Herald House, 1982).

2. The concepts of inclusion, control and affection can be found in William C. Schutz, *The Interpersonal Underworld* (Palo Alto: Science and Behavior Books, 1966).

extended periods of sobriety. They won't finesse a lapse into a full-blown relapse by concluding that they are no farther down the road to recovery than they were when their treatment began. Instead, they will credit themselves with the progress already made and accept the lapse, and the associated state-dependent feelings and thoughts. They are more likely to see their breach of sobriety for what it is: a slip with vivid recall due to biochemically and physiologically based state-dependent memories.

State-dependent learning is a key to understanding the progressive nature of addiction. We are told that if crack addicts or alcoholics return to drugs or booze after long periods of abstinence, it will be as though they never stopped using. Returning to the drug after a period of abstaining chemically unlocks the door to those frozen memories—feelings, smells, tastes, thoughts and behaviors. Until then, they were locked up by the brain's inability to retrieve the data.

State-dependent recall may occur when you walk into a room giving off a particular smell. You flash back to some early childhood experience. You see the place vividly. You remember immediately your earlier feelings. You are amazed by the clarity of the experience. You may even say to someone, "I haven't thought about this for years." This is a powerful phenomenon. If treatment professionals could come up with a way to block the client's state-dependent memories, to change their triggering effects, the addict might reenter the weakened grip of memories associated with compulsive drug-use. Then, a small breach of sobriety would not rekindle a compulsion to use the psychoactive substance.

Blocking State-Dependent Recall

Antabuse and Naltrexone. It is not the first dose of a drug that causes a full-blown relapse; it is the recall of the last ten thousand drinks or doses. It is not the one-time use of a crack or alcohol that causes an out-of-control relapse. The unlocking of the feelings, thoughts, and behaviors, through state-dependent recall, triggers the relapse. Before that first use, abstainers cannot recall *all* the feelings, thoughts and behaviors associated with their earlier drug-taking or drinking. The first dose awakens those sleeping memories. The first use brings it all back.

Antabuse is a drug that prevents someone from going into the state of recall that triggers a return to addiction. Antabuse causes a series of extremely unpleasant reactions in someone who ingests alcohol while Antabuse is still in the body. Prescribing the regular use of this drug is an attempt to prevent people from entering physiological states that access addictive thoughts and feelings. Naltrexone, a long-term narcotic antagonist, acts similarly. Narcotics are destroyed by Naltrexone, which works like little PacMen, gobbling up dope when it enters the system. This prevents drug users from becoming high and entering the state of mind they were in when compulsively using narcotics. It prevents the user from accessing state-dependent cues.

Behavioral Interventions. We are also working behaviorally to prevent state-dependent recall, transforming drug associated memories and feelings so they become benign. A good example of this *reframing* of state-dependent recall is seen in *deaddiction*, formally and technically called covert conditioning and desensitization. Desensitization therapy first induces imagery of drug-related scenes from the client's earlier life. A client in deep relaxation, or under hypnosis, recalls drug-associated events with remarkable clarity. When the client reports being aware of state-dependent cues to use drugs, we intervene with *thought stopping,* followed by covert positive reinforcement.

Covert positive reinforcement is simply having the client visualize a scene that is subjectively pleasing, immediately after imagining a behavior the therapist wants increased. It is operant positive reinforcement performed through visual imagery, deep relaxation, or hypnosis. For example, the therapist may instruct the client to visualize a scene wherein he is confronted with cocaine. The client is instructed to visualize saying no, rejecting the drug. The therapist immediately has the client imagine a beautiful beach scene or sunset, something pleasing. This reinforces the drug-rejecting behavior that has just occured in the client's visual imagery. The goal is to desensitize the client to the state-dependent trigger.

An example of covert negative reinforcement is somewhat different. Both negative and positive forms of covert reinforcement increase the frequency of the target behavior, but covert negative reinforcement does this through an escape paradigm. What this means is that the client escapes an uncomfortable situation by performing a positive behavior. For example, the therapist has the client imagine being surrounded by a roomful of cocaine. The client is asked to visualize the drugs located around him on tables, in cookers, and in pipes. The client becomes anxious and agitated. Now the therapist instructs the client to say no. Then the client is directed back into a relaxed state. The client learns that he can only escape the anxiety, the discomfort, the panic, by rejecting the drug.

The two types of covert conditioning can be combined into a counterconditioning paradigm. For example, the client is first brought to a relaxed state. He then visualizes a roomful of drugs. Anxiety soars. The therapist instructs the client to say no to the drugs (covert negative reinforcement) to stop the anxiety. Then the therapist introduces a pleasing visual imagery scene (covert positive reinforcement) to reinforce the rejection.

Through covert conditioning we alter the conditioned responses associated with a particular physiological state. Rather than allow the client to be reactive to established cues, we break up the chaining of these "triggers." When the client feels the anxiety of craving, drug use is no longer his only available response. Other responses become associated with that state. As therapists using covert conditioning, we water down the direct state-dependent association between psychoactive drug use and the thoughts, feelings, and reactive behaviors.

Consider a common stimulus response paradigm in drug addiction: *see drugs > feel craving > use drugs > decreased craving.* Through covert conditioning the above chain is broken. The result might be:

- sees drugs > no craving (*covert extinction or desensitization*)
- sees drugs > feels craving > says no > craving stops (*covert negative reinforcement*)
- sees drugs > says no > craving stops > sees self on a beautiful beach (*covert positive reinforcement*)

These are but a few examples of operant behavior therapy models to break up the *see drugs > feel craving > use drugs* chain.

Some useful work was done on this in Boston College in the late sixties and early seventies. There has been a resurgence of this technique among chemical dependency counselors in the late-eighties and its use should expand during the nineties.

Progression: A Continuum of Impairment

If we consider chemical dependency to be *an impairment caused by repeated, compulsive self-administration of drugs,* then we would expect to find a continuum of impairment, a progression of usage and we do. This continuum of impairment can be observed with crack, alcohol, benzos, opiates, inhalants, marijuana, and other psychoactive substances. Successful treatment disrupts this progression, at whatever level of drug involvement is displayed when the addict seeks help.

With crack cocaine, our early treatment encounters often involve persons who are at the lower end of the continuum of impairment. To illustrate, someone arrested for possession of marijuana has a problem with drugs. The problem is the police record and its consequences, not necessarily addiction. The treatment to disrupt the addictive progression should be educational, informing the client about addiction and the dangers associated with psychoactive chemicals. Solving the problem may not require abstinence from all psychoactive chemicals even if the goal of abstinence from marijuana and other illicit drugs would be socially desirable. It may be counterproductive to try to convince clients that they must never use a psychoactive chemical and remain "recovering" for life. This sentence might be all it would take to alienate clients from any further treatment.

Conversely, crack users who seek help and are obviously addicted need to adhere to the standard of total abstinence. They need to understand the progressive nature of addiction and to see ongoing recovery as a goal. They also need to learn that the ultimate goal of any treatment is mainstreaming back into society. Counselors who came into the chemical dependency treatment field by way of drug abuse treatment learned this the hard way. We sometimes worked successfully with abusers by setting goals of functionality. We even permitted controlled drinking by this population with some success. But when we tried the same approach with the addict, we saw many of them self-destruct on alcohol. Addicted persons need both the goals of total abstinence and of functionality.

The Merger of Alcohol and Drug Counseling

In the midseventies, there was a merger of the previously distinct professions of drug counselor and alcohol counselor. This difficult transition resulted in the professional category now known as the Chemical Dependency Counselor. The by-product of the merger of the two kinds of counselors into a single profession was greater uniformity in treatment and, eventually, a pervasive mind-set on addictions treatment, a generalized theory of addiction. The disease concept, already well-established in alcoholism treatment, began to dominate our thinking and discourse. Although many drug addiction counselors resisted designating addiction as a disease, most of them ultimately adopted this view. Still, some drug addiction counselors never fully agreed with this increasingly favored conception.

The predominant belief among alcoholism counselors was that recovery required total abstinence from alcohol. Their goal for clients was a lifetime status of ongoing recovery predicated upon this abstinence. Drug treatment professionals had different ideas. They saw the goal of treatment as functionality, not abstinence. They considered the addict someone who can recover, not a person who remains forever in a recovering state once treatment is completed. They characterized past clients who were

successful in treatment as "ex-addicts," no
addicts."

The difference in orientation between drug counselors
and their counterparts in the alcoholism field contrasted
the medical model of addiction (a primary, progressive,
terminal condition) with the social-behavioral model (the
last stop on a continuum of compulsive self-administration
of drugs on a continuum including use, abuse and addiction).

By the early 1980s, the merger of the drug and alcohol
treatment fields was complete. Counselors learned from
each other, but I think drug abuse counselors learned
more from alcohol counselors than vice versa. This is
because most of the clients being treated in the early
1980s were alcoholics. Another reason that the alcohol
orientation became dominant was that alcohol treatment
was the first to be marketed by hospitals and private
clinics. Alcoholism treatment programs portrayed themselves as "professional."

Drug abuse counselors working in this professional
milieu learned disease concepts. They learned the physiology of alcohol, the effects of alcohol on the family, and
about adult children of alcoholics. They began to understand codependency and enabling. They considered cross-
addictions and undertook relapse prevention planning.
They even understood alcohol as a drug. A vast amount of
information was offered to the field of drug addiction
treatment by those trained primarily in alcohol abuse and
alcoholism.

Crack Proves Resistant to Treatment

Then came the adolescent polydrug epidemic and the crack epidemic of the mid-1980s. Our treatment system, which had developed into a "Minnesota Model," based on The Hazelden Foundation's work with alcoholics, was now confronted with a group of clients who did not fit the model. The approaches that we had learned in the early 1980s, based on alcoholics, did not work with the new clients.

We admitted young crack addicts into our generic twenty-eight-day inpatient programs and used our techniques with them . . . without much success. We gave canned lectures on the physiological effects of drugs, teaching them about neurotransmitters and twin studies. We taught the slogans and sayings of recovery, yet clients left treatment prematurely (AMA) or completed inpatient services and self-destructed the first day they were out the door. We found ourselves using methods and techniques that weren't meeting the unique demands of crack addicts and polydrug-abusing adolescents. Counselors who had allowed themselves to believe they had put the lid on the black box of addiction now saw the box blow up in their faces.

Professional chemical dependency counselors began to say things like, "Those crack addicts never get better!" and "Those adolescents just haven't reached bottom yet; there's nothing we can do with them." As a profession we moved from the social-behavioral model in the 1970s, to a disease model in the early 1980s, to a blame-the-client-if-they-don't-get-better model in the late 1980s. The techniques

16

for working with drug abusers, which we learned in the 1970s, had become a lost art.

2

CRACK

The Addictive Complex

I was told a story about crack addicts by a good friend who happens to be a recovering addict. The story was about a man with severe headaches. He went to see a psychologist and was told that it was all psychological. He then went to see a psychiatrist who recommended that he take medication. Nothing seemed to help. Finally, he visited a neurologist with a good reputation for helping victims of severe headaches. The neurologist, after testing and CT scans, told the gentleman that his only hope was a brain transplant. The man was sent to a small room in the basement of the hospital to pick out a brain for the transplant operation.

As he walked into the dimly-lit basement he noticed a half-dozen tables scattered around the room. On each table, in bowls covered by bell jars, were brains. Each bell jar had two labels. One label gave the history of the brain; the other, its price. He was greeted by a salesman in a white lab coat. "May I help you?" asked the salesman. "No, I'm just looking." First he looked at a brain under a shiny new bell jar. It had belonged to a physicist; the price . . . twenty-five thousand dollars. "Quality brain," he thought, "but too much." The next brain belonged to an attorney. It looked good, but again the price of forty thousand dollars was a little more than he wanted to spend. Out of the corner of his eye, the shopper noticed a brain over in the corner. The bell jar covering it was dirty and dusty. Upon closer examination he noted that it had belonged to a crack addict. "How much for this one?" he asked. "Oh, that brain sells for one hundred thousand dollars." "My God," shouted the man, "the physicist's brain costs twenty-five thousand and the lawyer's brain is forty thousand. Why should I pay one hundred thousand dollars for a crack addict's brain?" "Well," responded the salesman, "it has never been used."

Counselors laugh at this because in some dark corner of our mind lives the thought that perhaps crack addicts—and maybe even alcoholics and opiate addicts—just don't use their heads. Still, we all know that there is a warehouse of information showing that addiction is far more complex and that treating this disorder demands all the creativity and intelligence we can find in ourselves. The crack cocaine addict is among the drug counselor's most challenging clients. It takes enormous skills to help crack-addicted clients overcome the vast and complex problems they present. Successful recovery is elusive and many counselors, if given the choice, would prefer working with other addictions.

A Client Hierarchy

Among chemical dependency counselors there is a tacit hierarchy of clients based on our judgment of who we believe will make it in treatment. Professionals draw an imaginary line between addictions on this continuum.

-Classic gamma alcoholics
-Other alcoholics
-Benzodiazepine addicts
-Other prescription drug addicts
---*Imaginary line*
-Opiate addicts
-Crack addicts

If given a choice of whom to work with, most chemical dependency counselors would choose cases above the imaginary line. There are some exceptions. Some chemical dependency counselors love the challenge of the bottom group and find the top group too boring, too compliant, too passive. But the average counselor's preferences coincide with the rankings of the CATOR reports, revealing that the highest success rates are for alcoholics; the lowest, for opiate and crack addicts.[1]

---

1. CATOR, the Chemical Abuse/Addiction Treatment Outcome Registry, is a service of the Ramsey Clinic, Department of Psychiatry, St. Paul, Minnesota. The reports I am referring to were available in 1988 on: adult outpatient treatment, adolescent treatment, and adult inpatient treatment. For more on the CATOR Reports, contact: CATOR, 17 West Exchange Street, St. Paul, MN 55102.

A frequent assumption is that those within the bottom group, crack and heroin addicts, are less likely to recover because they are less motivated, less sincere about recovery, more in denial, or more resistant. I disagree. I believe that they are less successful in treatment because we are less skillful in working with them. We have failed to develop and expand systems that are therapeutically appropriate for the unique needs of these clients. They are just as motivated as the other types of addicts, but are put into a healthcare system that is not designed to meet their needs.

It can be misleading to categorize addicts by the psychoactive substance they smoke, snort, shoot, or swallow. More critical factors than choice of drug divide them. The preferred (top) group uses legal substances while the bottom group uses illegal substances. Using illegal substances introduces a cluster of discriminating factors into treatment. Users of illegal drugs will be overrepresented by criminal, antisocial, immoral, and distasteful street behaviors that offend the average person and, at times, even empathic chemical dependency counselors.

The marketing of addiction treatment by hospitals and clinical centers has been good in some ways. When we as a society now think of alcoholics, we picture people with a biogenetic, intergenerational disease. Whether this characterization is scientifically valid or not, it is a humane, nonpunitive idea. But when we think of crack addicts, we don't always think first of someone with a disease, a person suffering from a biogenetic, intergenerational condition. We accept labels like "criminal," "socio-path," "amoral," and "egocentrically grandiose" within a case study. And while these terms may describe the behavior of some crack addicts, they also describe anyone else who has to interact in the illicit drug market to obtain a substance on the street. When some counselors discuss crack and heroin users, we hear things like, "they have no motivation." It takes a hell-of-a-lot of motivation to stand in the rain and snow for four hours, wearing wet tennis shoes, at three o'clock in the morning, in a dangerous part of town to buy a bag of smack or a piece of crack to take the sick away. This group is plenty motivated, but in a way vastly different from mainstream society.

I have often been asked if crack addicts are crazy people who happen also to use drugs. Casual observers say these addicts act so weird that they must have had some type of premorbid (before addiction) pathology. Some did, but not most. Many act insane within the confines of their addiction, but the lifestyle of maintaining a drug habit on the streets taught them these behaviors. If the most normal, average person in the world became crack addicted, lived on the streets, and was later inter-viewed, that normal, average person would seem crazy indeed. People do what they must to survive. To survive as a crack addict demands adaptation and accommodation. To the outsider, this adaptation looks like madness.

Differences Between Crack Addicts and Alcoholics

Unlike the average alcoholic, who is usually well socialized, employed, educated, and who could be the person next door, crack addicts often have developmental deficits. Some mainstream people have taken the dive due to drugs, but among crack addicts there is an overrepresentation of groups with developmental deficits, from the American underclass. Most crack addicts are not conventionally employed, not highly educated, and they live in difficult surroundings. This explains the change in attitudes toward the cocaine addict over the past ten years. When middle- and upper middle-class cocaine hydrochloride snorters were coming into treatment, counselors had few problems treating them. The difficulties started with the crack epidemic, which touched a different market.[2]

---

2. The TOPS report shows that the crack-addicted population is not representative of the general population in age, education, criminality, or work history. See R.L. Hubbard et al., *Drug Abuse Treatment: A National Study of Effectiveness* (Chapel Hill: University of North Carolina Press, 1989). The FY 1989-90 Florida Client-Oriented Data Acquisition Process (CODAP) report showed that recipients of drug abuse treatment services are unrepresentative of the general population, 66 percent male and 34 percent female; 48 percent white, 42 percent black, and 10 percent hispanic. The modal age group served was 25-34, representing 48 percent of the total. This age group represents less than 15 percent of the general population. Sixty percent had been arrested within the 24 months prior to treatment; 65 percent were unemployed. (Florida Department of Health and Rehabilitative Services, Alcohol and Drug Abuse Programs. "Client Admissions for Drug Abuse Treatment: FY 89-90." Tallahassee, FL.: March, 1991.)

Even mainstream people addicted to drugs are often undersocialized or have developmental deficits originating at the onset of their addiction. As chemical dependency professionals, we know that social and emotional development "freezes" at the level of psychosocial development where compulsive, self-administered, drug use begins.

There is a third important distinction between crack users and alcoholics. The alcohol addict, using a legal drug, is unlikely to be referred for treatment before reaching a high level of dysfunction. Generally, alcoholics who enter treatment are in the middle or later stages of addiction. Illicit drug users, due to criminal justice interventions, often enter treatment programs before having reached the high degree or intensity of dysfunction of the licit drug user. The crack user entering treatment may be at an earlier stage of dependency. The strategies and clinical interventions that we have developed for the middle- and late-stage alcoholic may not be applicable to the early-stage, early-intervened, crack user. In my experience, it takes more finesse or seduction to treatment to work with the early-stage addict than the later-stage addict.

When considering these two groups, alcoholic and pre-scription addicts versus the crack addict or the opiate addicts, we need to see the distinction in terms of: (1) primary culture versus subculture; (2) socialized versus undersocialized with developmental deficits; and, (3) later-stage versus early-stage intervention. By reframing our thinking this way, we accomplish two things. First, we don't classify high and low potential for success solely on the basis of the nature of the psychoactive substance, ignoring client characteristics. Second, we are encouraged to develop precise behavioral strategies to remedy specific client problems.

Crack cocaine users require treatment programs that habilitate and socialize, not the one-shot, high-intensity learning experience characteristic of alcohol dependency treatment. Programs addressing the fundamental habilitation issues and socialization issues raised by crack addicts must provide long-term, repeated exposure to life skills. Through psychoeducational seminars and behaviorally oriented skill-building sessions, developmental deficits can be remediated. Crack addicts who have never been socialized into the mainstream culture, clients who seem to have been raised by wolves, can still, in this way, learn the skills necessary to function in America. We must accept and act according to this prescription or suffer the alternative: a siege mentality and an ever-increasing prison population.

Why Is Crack So Addictive?

Years ago, we believed that certain drugs were more addictive than others. It was once thought that heroin was the most addictive drug, far more addictive than alcohol, marijuana, or cocaine. The heroin user had only to do it once to become addicted for life. Reporting a social heroin user would have been like reporting an alien in a UFO. I once believed that it was impossible to become addicted to marijuana. Many of us smoked it when we were growing up. We believed it couldn't be that bad if we used it. We know today that this is false.

A client came into my office one day and told me that she was a marijuana addict. I questioned this, but I tried to act like a good counselor, understanding and professional. I asked her why she thought she was addicted to marijuana. "Well," she said, "I smoke pot a lot, and think about it all the time. Two weeks ago, my parents went on vacation. They left me some money to get by on . . . but I spent it all on pot the first week. When the money ran out, I wanted more marijuana, but I was broke. I remembered my mom and dad had a wall safe in the house. So, a friend of mine and me dynamited the wall safe. We got the money and bought more marijuana. My mom and dad will be home this weekend, but what can I do? I'm out of pot, and the living room wall is blown up." Wow! She exhibited *loss of control*. She had *compulsive thoughts*. She *continued use despite consequences*. I had to accept that it was possible to be addicted to marijuana.

Addiction Proneness. Chemical dependency counselors believe the prevalence rate of addiction, the ratio of addicts to users of psychoactive substances, to be approximately 1:10. This means that ten percent of the people who use a psychoactive substance will become addicted. My guess is that this statistic came from the prevalence rate for alcoholism among alcohol users. The average prevalence rate for alcoholism is one-in-ten but it varies considerably when you look at selected groups. Addiction rates are different for children of alcoholics, persons with emotional problems, socially oppressed or disadvantaged groups, and among cultures that condone or discourage the use of beverage alcohol.

The crack epidemic forced us to rethink and research the rate of addiction among persons who use a specific psychoactive substance. Today, experts make varied claims about the addiction rate for crack. Some experts recite the one in ten ratio. Others state flatly that, like heroin years ago, everyone who uses crack becomes addicted.[3] I estimate an addiction rate for crack of 40 percent plus-or-minus, depending upon the effects of factors such as cost and the intensity of marketing.

Dr. Arnold Washton of the *Cocaine Hotline*, first presented this information in the mid-1980s.[4] He cited three factors that influence addiction proneness, and I have since added a fourth. These factors indicate how

---

3. Dr. Ray Wise, a Montreal researcher in the area of cocaine, is often credited with first expressing the incredible addictive potential of crack cocaine. Few experts would say that everyone who uses cocaine will become addicted, but many argue with the National Institute on Drug Abuse statistics that indicate approximately 25 percent of users become addicts. Treatment professionals believe the one-in-four ratio is low.

4. I heard Dr. Washton speak at the SECAD conference in Atlanta in 1985. Dr. Washton has since authored several articles on cocaine dependency and treatment, including the landmark paper: "Crack: The Newest Lethal Addiction," *Medical Aspects of Human Sexuality*, 20 (September 1986):49-55. Also see Arnold Washton and Mark Gold, *Cocaine: A Clinician's Handbook* (NY: The Guilford Press, 1987).

addictive a drug is for an individual. The addiction proneness factors are:

1. Speed of onset
2. Degree of pleasure when using
3. Degree of discomfort when stopping
4. The duration of psychoactive effects.

The *speed of onset* is the length of time it takes from ingesting (snorting, smoking, drinking, or shooting) the substance to feeling the effects. The faster one feels the effects of using a drug, the more addictive it is. This is a basic principle from learning theory. The faster one reinforces a behavior, the more likely it is the behavior will occur again. If a teacher gives a piece of candy to students each time they raise their hands in response to a question, the classroom will be filled with children with raised hands. If I ingest a psychoactive drug and it takes three weeks to feel the effects, I get little reinforcement. If I drink this potion and feel euphoric immediately, I will want another sip right away.

It takes about twenty minutes to feel the pharmacological effects of alcohol. There are some effects that occur sooner that reinforce the actual act of pouring the substance into the mouth, the burning, the grimace when gulping the alcohol, the glow in the throat and gut, but the actual psychoactive effect takes time. These secondary effects are important because they chain together to form a reinforcer for consumption.

When heroin is injected it takes about fifteen seconds to change the user's mood. Reinforcement for all the behaviors preceding the injection is quick, and therefore strong. The feeling of euphoria from the injection reinforces the behaviors of putting the dope in the cooker, heating the dope, drawing the heroin up into a syringe and tying off, injecting, and booting the drug. With crack cocaine, the speed of onset effect is extreme. It takes seven seconds for the crack smoker to feel the effects of the drug. Within seven seconds, the user is reinforced for the preceding behaviors: putting the crack into a pipe, striking a match or lighter, and sucking in the vapors. This is almost instant reinforcement. It is easy to understand why crack addicts report a strong compulsion to use. It is a behavioral compulsion. There are some biochemical factors involved, but the basic paradigm is behavioral.

The second factor that determines the addiction potential of a drug is the *degree of pleasure* derived when using it. Pleasure is an increase in enjoyable sensations or the masking of painful ones. Some people find pleasure in a drug because it produces euphoria, but others find pleasure in a drug because it extinguishes their constant pain. By learning how much pleasure is derived from a drug, how much better than normal the feeling when using, one can see how addictive the drug is for that individual.

For example, consider a person scoring nine on a ten-point feelgood scale. When this person uses a drug, he or she can only experience an increase of ten percent from the baseline level, a reinforcement worth one point we might say. Suppose someone with a score of four on our ten-point feelgood scale jumps to a ten when using. By going from a normal state of four to a ten, the person derives a six-point reinforcement instead of a one point reinforcement, a sixty percent upward shift. This is the emotional or psychological aspect of addiction and addiction proneness. The better one feels about oneself initially, the less reinforcement potential a drug has. This is the foundation of prevention efforts in the United States. By increasing a person's feelings of satisfaction and self-worth, therapists decrease the reinforcement potential of psychoactive substances. The illustration shows that persons with low self-concepts derive relatively greater pleasure from using psychoactive substances than do people who feel good about themselves. Therefore, those with low self-concepts are overrepresented among those who progress from social user to addict.

The third factor determining the addiction proneness of a drug is how much *pain or discomfort the user experiences when discontinuing* it. The casual user who discontinues alcohol after a night of revelry feels a hangover. This hangover is unlikely to be painful enough to create a state wherein use is maintained to escape discomfort. Some hung over drinkers take some "hair of the dog that bit 'um" to escape feeling bad, but most don't. This changes dramatically as one progresses into alcoholism. When drinking starts to provide more than casual enjoyment, when it is used to relieve pressure and stress and to reduce psychic pain, then the discomfort associated with discontinuance is more than a simple hangover. Discontinuing alcohol may allow the resurgence of psychic pain, compounded with guilt, remorse and feelings of failure, induced by the drinking itself. If the alcohol user has developed a significant degree of tolerance for the drug, terminating its use may bring on more than a simple hangover. It may cause shakes, seizures, hallucinations and delirium tremens. Those symptoms can be a compelling motivation to have another drink.

With crack cocaine, the subjective discomfort accompanying discontinuance of the drug involves shakiness, depression, suicidal feelings, suspicion, paranoia, and an overwhelming feeling of despair. When people reach such a high degree of discomfort while knowing that using crack will make them feel better in seven seconds, they will use again. Each such use reinforces the compulsion.

The fourth factor affecting addiction proneness is the *duration of a drug's psychoactive effects*. For example, assume there are two different drugs. Drug A has a rapid onset, creates a high degree of pleasure when used, leads to a high degree of displeasure when discontinued and maintains the pleasurable experience for 12 hours after each administration. Drug B has a rapid onset, creates a high degree of pleasure when used, brings on a high degree of displeasure when discontinued, but maintains the pleasurable experience for five minutes after each administration. Which drug has a higher addiction potential? Drug B. The user of Drug A self-administers (shoots, snorts, smokes, or drops) once every twelve hours. The user of Drug B self-administers every five minutes and thus has more repeated exposure to the substance. The user is driven more often to buy, prepare, and administer the drug. Drug B, due to its short duration of psychoactive effects, requires closely spaced, repeated exposures. We know that the more often one repeats a behavior, the faster it becomes a habit.

In the above example, Drug A could be ice, and Drug B, crack cocaine. Ice will be a tremendously abused drug in America, but I do not think it will produce a large number of addicts. The effects of using a single dose of ice last so long that people will burn out on it while still in the abuse stage. This happened with the meth-amphetamine IV epidemic of the 1960s. Speed freaks realized, after a few exposures to the drug, that *meth* is toxic stuff. Many chose to discontinue it while they were still abusers with voluntary control. Some crossed the line and became addicted; and this will happen with ice, too, but it will never approach the addictiveness of crack cocaine. Ice will, however, undoubtedly have a significant impact on the criminal justice system. It is illegal, and it is a long-acting central nervous system stimulant that causes bizarre, antisocial behavior. But I do not think ice will cause the addiction epidemic forecast by the media.

The fact that these addiction proneness factors in-fluence a drug's addictive potential, suggests that addiction is much more than a biogenetically predisposed disease. It is a behavioral compulsion based on the dynamics of positive reinforcement: speed of onset, pleasure above baseline when using, and repeated exposures. Addiction involves punishment and negative reinforcement, discom-fort on discontinuance, with the escape paradigm of continued use, working together in a powerful counter-conditioning design, the most effective design for changing

33

human behavior. Addiction obeys the laws governing the dynamics of human behavior. Though some persons are at higher risk due to greater sensitivity factors, all humans are at risk. No one is immune.

What About the Person?

Some drugs are addictive due to the speed of onset, the pleasure they create when active, the discomfort they create when discontinued, and the frequency of repeated administrations. The state of a person's self-concept often dictates his degree of addiction proneness. People with low self-concepts receive relatively more reinforcement from a pleasure producer than do those with higher self-concepts. But some people are prone to addiction due to other factors. Genetic factors, cultural encouragement of excessive consumption of psychoactive substances, socio-economic conditions, psychic pain, and an individual's unique biochemistry are all factors that influence addictive risk.

A colleague and expert on addictions, C.C. Nuckols, developed a graphic display depicting the factors that influence the likelihood of becoming a drug or alcohol user, abuser or addict.[5] I merged his model with with the Public Health Model of Disease to create Figure 1, below.

---

5. Cardwell C. Nuckols has been a forerunner in providing training and authoring materials on the treatment of cocaine dependency. See his book *Cocaine: From Dependency to Recovery* (Blude Ridge Summit, PA: HSI/TAB Books, 1989).

Figure 1. The Interaction of Consumption Rate and Sensitivity in Determining Addiction

high

C O N S U M P T I O N			
	abuse/addiction	addiction	addiction
	abuse	abuse/addiction	addiction
	use	abuse	abuse/addiction

low SENSITIVITY TO SUBSTANCE **high**
(genetics/cultural/social/psychic pain/physical pain)

Figure 1 shows that if a person consumes small amounts of psychoactive substances and has low sensitivity to developing addiction, that person probably will stay in the user category indefinitely. However, consider those who consume small amounts of psychoactive substances but who have a high sensitivity. Assume they are genetically linked to parents who are alcoholics and are raised in a family culture that encourages excessive drug use. Further, assume that they may not have been exposed to religious sanctions against excessive drug use and that they live in a community where recreation and socialization revolve around drug or alcohol consumption. They have an

35

intense psychic pain or chronic physical pain. Those people are extremely susceptible to becoming addicts, even with moderate-to-low consumption. Biogenetic factors may increase or decrease a person's probability of becoming addicted, but there are social and behavioral factors that determine if, when, and how the addiction will strike and the addictive potential of a particular drug.

THE DISEASE CONCEPT

Does It Apply to Crack?

I worked in the counseling field for years, never knowing that addiction was a disease. My clients who got better never knew they had a disease. Was I just lucky? Was it spontaneous remission? I had become a successful chemical dependency counselor, but deep down I really did not know what the disease concept meant.

At first I felt like I was the only professional in the field who didn't have the answers. I questioned my competence. I was thrown into an identity crisis, wondering what I really knew about addiction. I feverishly read books on the disease concept. I attended weekend and evening workshops on the disease concept. I viewed most of the films. Finally, I realized that the disease concept, as presented in the field of addictions, was inherently unclear, ambiguous and contradictory.

The "X" Factor

At one level, the disease concept of addiction means that all addicts are genetically predisposed to drugs and alcohol due to an "X Factor." The X Factor is only identified after addiction has become evident. There is no screening test, physical or psychometric, to detect reliably the *predisposition* among persons who have yet to become involved with drinking or drug taking. Moreover, the idea that all addicts are genetically predisposed seems vague and implausible when you consider that many people who are addicted have no evidence of alcohol or drug addiction in their family history.

The conventional response to this troubling paradox is to contend that the genetic predisposition is intergenerational. The X Factor may have originated several generations earlier, in a distant relative beyond the reach of family memory or historical record. Others defend the disease concept, when challenged this way, by saying that although present alcoholics or addicts may have no alcoholics or drug addicts in their lineage, there may have been workaholics, overeaters, gamblers, or compulsively religious people in their family tree. Any of these could have had the disease, the X factor, now manifesting itself as a psychoactive chemical addiction. The trouble with this explanation is that everyone has a parent, grandparent or great-grandparent who has overworked, overeaten, over-gambled or overprayed. Do we all have the X Factor?

To many the disease concept means the addict-alcoholic has a progressive terminal condition with a predictable outcome: insanity or death. We are also told that the disease concept means that once you are an addict, you will follow the progression to its conclusion, death, unless someone or something intervenes. "Once an addict, always an addict," they say. If this is correct, how do some addicts manage to quit on their own?

In response to the paradox of the addict who successfully self-intervenes in his addiction, some experts claim he was never addicted. When asked why some addicts can return to occasional controlled use of psychoactive substances, the response is that they too were never really addicted. This contention is so strongly defended that one of its advocates told me that a colleague who shot heroin for twenty years, spending six years in prison because of shooting dope and losing his family in the process, never was an addict because he now has eight years of narcotics abstinence but drinks a few beers a month. This is impossible if you have the Disease of Addiction.

The biogenetic-biochemical disease concept model is typically presented in biophysical terms that most people in the profession do not understand. The average counselor does not understand chemistry, biology, or physiology at the level that the biochemical-biogenetic disease concept proponents present their arguments. Counselors cannot challenge what they don't understand, nor can they fully understand its implications for their practice. Dazzled by authoritative expertise, counselors accept the disease concept without fully understanding its implications *and limitations*.

Exponents defend the disease concept by citing studies of twins, THIQs, and rats that drink alcohol. The argument that alcoholism is strictly a biogenetic disease is often supported by what many professionals call the twin studies. This refers to research involving twins separated through adoption: the Denmark study[1] and the Sweden study.[2] These studies present evidence of genetic predisposition to alcoholism among *some* populations.[3] This research does not infer that genetics are the exclusive etiology of addition. It is only one of many interactive factors. Granted, there is evidence that among some samples of some populations there exists neuropsychological differences and biochemical differences between those who develop alcoholism and those who do not. But it is an oversimplification to say that there is a single, uniform etiology of addiction.

It is unfortunate that in the United States the disease concept has been interpreted to mean that the biogenetics of the host, the addict, is the major contributing cause of

---

1. D. W. Goodwin, F. Schulsinger, L. Hermansen, S. B. Guze, and G. Winokur, "Alcohol Problems in Adoptees Raised Apart from Biological Parents," *Archives of General Psychiatry* 28, (1973): 238-243.

2. C. R. Cloninger, M. Bohman and S. Sigvardsson, "Inheritance of Alcohol Abuse: Cross Fostering Analysis of Adopted Men," *Archives of General Psychiatry* 38, (1981): 861-868.

3. The research methodology has been critiqued in John S. Searles, "The Role of Genetics in the Pathogenesis of Alcoholism," *Journal of Abnormal Psychology* 97, no. 2(1988): 153-167.

addiction, discounting the role of the agent, beverage alcohol, or the environment. "To overextend genetic thinking so as to deny these personal and social meanings in drinking does a disservice to the social sciences, to our society, and to alcoholics and others with drinking problems."[4]

Not long ago, a film entitled *Disease Concept of Alcoholism* was routinely shown in treatment programs in the United States. In this film, a strong argument for the disease concept was presented by a physician who alluded to biochemical research on alcoholism. It was claimed that the brain of an alcoholic is different from that of a nonalcoholic. The alcoholic brain allegedly generates THIQs, which increase a person's compulsion to drink beverage alcohol. Even rats who hate to have a drink will crave booze when injected with these THIQs and THQs, by-products of alcohol metabolism. A frequent interpretation of this film by counselors is that it proves that the etiology of alcoholism is strictly biochemical, hence, is an uncontrollable disease in which the victim or society plays no role in development. This can be a counterproductive assumption because it minimizes the interactive social, cultural, psychological and developmental factors that contribute to the prevalence of a disease.

To say that, because genetics has been shown to be one factor in the prevalence of addiction, it is the etiological cause is inaccurate. Genetics has a role in the intel-

---

4. S. Peele. "The Implications and Limitations of Genetic Models of Alcoholism and Other Addictions," *Journal of Studies on Alcohol* 47, no. 1(1986): 63-71.

ligence, personality, and therefore, indirectly, the behavior of all humans.[5] Genetics tends to influence intelligence and personality to varying degrees, thirty to seventy percent depending on the research study.[6] Although champion marathon runners, individuals with high IQs, and alcoholics may be overrepresented by families-of-origin with those traits, it does not indicate absolute determinism, nor does it indicate that environmental factors have no significant influence.

The biochemical-biogenetic disease concept implies that total responsibility for the individual's addiction lies within the cell, its chromosomes and DNA. This theory fails to acknowledge the importance of the role of cultural-social-environmental issues or even the pharmacology of the drug. Failing to explain why many people with chemical dependency problems show no evidence of any genetic predisposition, the model subtly encourages quasi-moralistic judgments about the fundamental nature of people who become addicted. Is the assumption that they are the ones

---

5. T.J. Bouchard, Jr., "Twins Reared Together and Apart: What They Tell Us About Human Diversity," in S.W. Fox, ed., *Individuality and Determinism: Chemical and Biological Bases* (New York: Plenum Press, 1982), 147-178.

6. There are hundreds of studies supporting the role of genetics in intelligence. The field of behavioral genetics has explored the influence of genetics on intelligence through large sample, well controlled research. Twin studies are often used to assess the relative strength of nature and nurture in human development. T. Adler, "Seeing Double?" *The Monitor* 22 (January 1991):1.

who, if not genetically predisposed, are morally weak, lazy or antisocial?

Diseased: All or Only Some?

In 1986, I participated in the Moscow Soviet-American Conference on Alcoholism. During the conference, an American asked a Soviet narcologist if the Soviets accept the disease concept of addiction. The Soviet narcologist responded, "First, I do believe that some alcoholics have a disease. You know that the disease concept is based on alcoholism, not on addiction. To generalize, and assume that all addictions are a disease, is a little premature." Surprised by this the American asked, "What do you mean . . . 'some alcoholics have a disease'?" The Soviet replied, "The problem is that people talk a lot about the disease concept without having read Jellenick's book." He was right. Of the Americans attending the conference, few had read Jellenick's book, *The Disease Concept of Alcoholism.*[7] Jellenick states that, of the various types of alcoholics, *some have a disease*. Not all alcoholics, only some.

So, some of my clients had the Disease of Addiction, and some didn't. This helped me understand why some clients seemed possessed, so much that a teaspoon of alcohol could trigger self-destruction, and others seemed more in control of themselves. But I was still confused

---

7. E.M. Jellinek, *The Disease Concept of Alcoholism* (New Haven: New Haven Hillhouse Press, 1960): 36-39.

about why the field did not call alcoholism a bad habit and let it go at that.

As a drug counselor, I had learned to think of addiction as a bad habit. Bad habits are caused by being positively reinforced for repeatedly doing something socially unacceptable or self-destructive, until the behavior becomes automatic. In treating clients who have bad habits, we teach them good habits and create an environment where their bad habits are no longer reinforced. My bad habit theory of addiction implied that anyone can develop the problem. It implied that the bad habit is changeable. It implied that the behavior is learned and that it is controllable, even if controlling it means stopping entirely. It implied that the habit is a continuum of impairment and that there are degrees of compulsivity, from weak to potent. Many people have bad habits. Some habits are more destructive than others and some people are gripped more strongly by their bad habits. Some have progressed farther into their bad habit than others. Why call this process a disease?

The Appeal of the Disease Concept. One reason Americans term addiction a disease is that it is consistent with our culture. Americans seem convinced that the only acceptable excuse for functioning at less than one hundred percent of adequacy is illness. Imagine asking your boss for the day off because you feel overwhelmed and isolated. You'd better say you're sick. A myth we live with is that the only excuse for nonoptimum functioning is sickness. Any other reason labels the person lazy, antisocial, or bad. Awarding the status of disease to addiction has the latent function of reducing moralistic judgments and it encourages a positive and sympathetic response to addicts by society. The disease concept of addiction also functions as a marketing tool to encourage people to seek counseling services without feeling stigmatized.

The Agent, the Host and the Environment

The Disease of Addiction is presented as atypical. We don't conceptualize crack addiction or alcoholism the same way we conceptualize other diseases. A friend and professional colleague, Bill Miller, alerted me to this. Other diseases are conceptualized in terms of three elements: the agent, the host and the environment. With the disease of addiction, we look almost exclusively at the host, the addict.

When considering other diseases we look first at the actual agent, the virus or the bacteria that infects the host. In the disease of alcoholism, the *agent* is alcohol or ethanol, a chemically dangerous toxin. The agent is inherently poisonous, one of the few toxins that affects and destroys almost every system in the host. How often when we speak publicly about alcoholism do we address the toxic effects of alcohol itself? But alcohol itself causes alcoholism just as often as do some vague biogenetically transmitted predisposers.

Once the disease agent is identified and its role understood, we study the environment in which the disease occurs. Different environments produce different rates of infection or contagion. Applying this to alcoholism, we see it occurring more frequently in societies that tolerate excessive use, that attach positive social value to drinking and that promote the open use of alcohol. How often, when speaking to church groups and civic organizations, do we focus on the role of society and our communities in causing alcoholism? Yet societal norms cause alcoholism as much, if not more than, some nebulous THIQ does.

To fully explain alcoholism, or any addiction, in terms of the disease concept, we should consider the agent (alcohol), the host (the person who drinks), and the environment (the society in which the use occurs). In a society with a free enterprise system, a proprietary health-care system and a billion-dollar liquor industry, there are financial interests at stake, incentives for focusing on the sick individual instead of the substance or the environment.

Counselors continue to have difficulty accepting the disease concept as a basis for treating addiction to crack cocaine. I struggled with this for many years, finally combining the disease concept and the "Minnesota Model" with the social-behavioral orientation. Integrating the two creates a more adequate foundation for working with crack addicts than either does alone. By studying social and behavioral models of addiction we understand "why" certain drugs are more addictive than others. And we understand why certain people are more susceptible to addiction.

The crack epidemic has made us reconsider how we conceptualize addiction. We have begun to move toward a true disease concept with cocaine addiction. We talk about the drug cocaine hydrochloride and explain why it is so powerful. We teach that cocaine is dangerous for more reasons than its addictive potential. Each time a person uses it, the drug causes physiological damage to many organs. We also consider the host, explaining the effects of cocaine on the brain, the behavioral compulsions associated with the fast onset of the high, and the dopamine depletion. We acknowledge the environment's role. We tell people that even occasional use of cocaine is abuse, and that there is no socially acceptable use. We have even gone so far as to restrict the television networks' use of cocaine humor. It isn't funny. We take cocaine addiction seriously, intervening on the three elements of the disease of cocaine addiction: the agent (cocaine hydrochloride), the host (the human being) and the environment (our society). We approach the crack epidemic from a genuine disease model.

Nicotine addiction is another example of the power of a disease concept when presented in its entirety. We, as a nation, are aggressively intervening in cigarette smoking. We are looking at the agent (cigarettes, tar, nicotine, carbon monoxide), the host (the smoker), and the environment (airplanes, work environments, passive inhalation research). Society is addressing all three aspects of the disease. We have established the goal of a smoke-free America. It is a great plan with a comprehensive focus.

The Soviets adopted a three-pronged approach to the disease of alcoholism. They limited access to the agent (alcohol) by raising its price. For the host (humans), they set up comprehensive prevention, education and treatment systems. As for the environment, they restructured the parks and clubs where people commonly consume alcohol. Vodka shops and bars were replaced with nonalcoholic beverage shops and soft drink machines. The U.S.S.R. began nondrinking clubs where people could socialize without alcohol.

Is It a Disease, or What?

Addiction to crack cocaine, characterized by loss of control, continued use despite consequences and compulsive preoccupation of thought, is a disease in the truest sense of the word. It is caused by an agent, with the host's susceptibility determined by genetic and emotional factors. Its prevalence is influenced by the environment—the cultural norms surrounding the substance's availability and sanctions governing its use and abuse. Crack addiction is a progressive disease if no changes occur within the agent (consumption rate), within the host (physically, emotionally, behaviorally), or within the environment (availability, cost, consumption norms).

Crack addiction is a disease that can be controlled by interventions that target more than just the behavior of the host, reducing access to the substance, developing anticonsumption norms, and reducing the community's tolerance for drug abuse. The three-pronged approach to the agent, the host, and the environment is the appropriate model for disease control with crack cocaine addiction.

My optimism for controlling this addiction may seem to contradict the Twelve-Step program belief that crack addicts are powerless over crack and alcoholics are powerless over alcohol. It does not conflict. Crack addicts are powerless over crack, but not their addiction to crack. By controlling their drugging, by learned abstinence, the addicts do have power over the addiction. This is the Twelve-Step approach, a Zen paradox: The best way to become strong over crack addiction is to allow yourself to be weak. The best way to become addiction free is to allow yourself to be an addict.

I'M JUST AN ABUSER

. . . Not an Addict

People don't become addicts overnight, and there are no clear lines separating users, abusers, and addicts. Addiction can be charted as a *continuum of impairment*. Glatt's curve of alcoholism (the progression) clearly shows that alcoholism is an incremental, evolutionary process, not a sudden phase shift from abuse to addiction.[1] Early definitions of addiction attempted to draw a clear line between addiction and other degrees and types of involvement with substances of abuse.[2] For years, from the early 1930s to 1960s, it was generally accepted that addiction was a

---

1. M. M. Glatt, *Alcoholism* (London: Hodder and Stoughton, 1982).

2. J. W. Dykens and G. D. Hiswander, "The Treatment of Drug Addiction" in *The Therapist's Handbook*, ed. B. J. Wolman. (New York: Van Nostrand Reinhold): 430-442.

condition characterized by tolerance to a drug and withdrawal upon discontinuance of that drug.

Jellinek, who had significant influence upon World Health Organization committees in the 1950s, moved professional thinking from the dichotomous model of addiction (abuse or addiction) to a model that conceptualizes addiction as degrees of personal and social impairment along a continuum from experimentation to use, abuse, and, finally, addiction. Unfortunately, we as a profession have dichotomized abuse and addiction for the past twenty years.

The old definitions of addiction represented an attempt at drawing a clear line between addiction and other degrees and types of involvements with substances of abuse. They stated that when there is tolerance and withdrawal, there is addiction. This definition proved inadequate because some drug users displayed patterns of compulsivity and destructiveness without developing tolerance and without experiencing medically definable withdrawal symptoms.

When cocaine first became popular, many people said it was nonaddictive because the user did not experience the same withdrawal as the alcoholic or the opiate dependent. When the crack or cocaine hydrochloride addict stopped using, withdrawal was not a medically definable withdrawal. There were no DT's, cramping, vomiting or other significant signs. The medical professionals claimed that cocaine abusers really didn't have withdrawal. Counselors saw something different. We witnessed addicts blow their brains out from the depression triggered when cocaine was discontinued. We realized that suicide is a significant withdrawal symptom. It told us cocaine is addictive.

The standard by which we define addicts usually distinguishes between abusers and addicts. This can be a dangerous mistake. The implication is that abusers are less dysfunctional than the addict. However, a vast number of problems associated with substance abuse originate with abusers. When someone gets into a car drunk and runs over a five-year-old child, does it matter if the driver is an abuser or an addict? When a spouse comes home high and beats the children, does it matter if that spouse is addicted or a user? We have made some big mistakes by focusing treatment on the addict, while tolerating the abuser and the user. We think the addict has a disease and needs treatment, but tolerate the occasional use of illegal drugs such as marijuana and cocaine because social users hurt no one but themselves, we claim.

At a party, several professionals were snorting coke in a back room. They invited me, and I was outraged. They called me a prude. They claimed to be social weekend users and their use did not interfere with anything. They could see nothing wrong with episodic use of an illegal drug, since they were only social users, not addicts.

Shortly after that incident, I heard a story about an arrest in Miami. A woman was charged with smuggling cocaine. She was hired in a South American country to carry a baby through customs into the United States. The baby had been killed, hollowed out, stuffed with cocaine, sewn up, and wrapped in a blanket so the woman could carry this apparently sleeping child through customs. When someone says using cocaine nonaddictively doesn't hurt anyone, I remember that baby who was sacrificed for the financial greed of smugglers and the drug hunger of social users. Illegal drug use is not a victimless crime. We all feel the impact!

When I was training in the West Indies, a workshop participant told me they define drug abuse as any use of an illegal substance. When anyone in the society uses any illegal drug, they are thought to be contributing to the disintegration of the quality of life for all in that society.

It's Not My Fault; I Have an Addictive Personality!

In many textbooks on addiction, there are sections on the addictive personality, the premorbid pathology that causes a person to become addicted. I believe that the existence of measurable and consistent differences in personality profiles between crack addicts and nonaddicts is a myth erected on weak research, bolstered by professional tradition, and reinforced by our spontaneous reactions to crack-addicted clients whose lifestyles often differ markedly from our own.

The concept of the addictive personality originated among researchers who set out to find if there was a particular type of person who was at risk for becoming addicted to drugs and alcohol. Interest in this question stemmed from a concern for prevention. If the alcoholic or drug addict had a measurably different personality, it might be possible to intervene earlier in the progression of addiction, perhaps even before an individual began experimenting with drugs. Also, there was and continues to be an interest in the underlying, premorbid dynamics that cause addiction. Knowing more about these personality dynamics could affect the nature and effectiveness of treatment.

When researchers packed up their *Minnesota Multiphasic Personality Inventories* and other tests to measure pathology, they went to places where drug addicts and alcoholics were easily identifiable. Where did researchers forty years ago find people willing to identify themselves as drug addicts and alcoholics? Prisons and mental hospitals. Although the subjects of these studies were addicts, an important covariate was overlooked when interpreting the results. People in prisons and mental hospitals are usually criminal, insane, or both. Addiction itself is rarely a sufficient reason to confine people to these facilities. If the researchers had studied addicts and alcoholics in schools, hospitals and businesses, the resulting addictive personality profile and the image of the addictive personality would have appeared different.

People with emotional problems do have a higher propensity toward crack addiction and other dependencies. But this can be explained by something more simple and more tangible than hypothetical constructs such as a *premorbid, addictive personality*. Emotional problems are often evident among crack addicts because this is the pain from which the chemical provides temporary relief.

Another flaw in the research defining the addictive personality is that it is correlational, not experimental, and therefore the results cannot be used to support the statement that an addictive personality *causes* addiction. An experimental research design would measure the personality types of individuals *before* exposure to drugs or alcohol, monitor the exposure, and at some later date calculate and compare addiction rates for the presumed nonaddictive and addictive personalities. There are always economic, political, and ethical questions surrounding experimental research on humans, especially when the treatments are potentially harmful. Rather than confront these problems, psychological researchers usually probe correlations, consistencies between psychological test results and after-the-fact measures of addiction. Even so, if a study is correlational and addicts display a much higher score on Factor X than nonaddicts, it doesn't prove that Factor X caused their addiction.

Deceptive Similarities. Our acceptance of the addictive personality explanation is subtly reinforced by the clients we see. Crack addicts *seem* to have similar personalities, to be more alike than different. They act alike; they say the same things; they have the same issues in counseling. Their apparent similarities in personality are primarily due to two simple facts: 1) their parallel lifestyles; and, 2) the targeted marketing of the drug.

First, crack addicts all have been living similar life-styles. They experience the same challenges out on the streets and have adapted similarly. They typically have an external locus of control, meaning they tend to try controlling externals instead of controlling themselves. This is common among addicts. It comes from a universal need for a sense of control in our lives. If we can't control ourselves, we try to control others. Crack addicts typically are suspicious, guarded and sometimes paranoid. The drug contributes to this. Living and surviving in a hostile, criminal environment reinforces this. Crack addicts all seem immoral. If living means performing any behavior to survive, one will do some very extreme, and sometimes immoral, things.

Secondly, crack addicts who enter programs are over-represented by similar people due to the marketing of crack cocaine to specifically targeted groups. Currently, the targeted markets are inner-city, black and hispanic, often those who belong to the underclass of America. They appear to be similar because they have been socialized in the same manner. They often come from the same subcommunity. They experienced the frustrations and roadblocks common to an underclass. However, this is changing. With crack cocaine expanding to the white, suburban market, we expect to see more heterogeneity among our clients.

The Quest for the Test

As discussed in the previous chapter, there is the belief that some people are predisposed to the disease of addiction. What if a test were available that would identify those who would be at high risk of addiction if they experimented with drugs? That is the hope of those who endorse social using, the quest for the test.

The quest for the test involves finding a test to determine at birth or at a young age if a person is predisposed to alcoholism, or drug addiction. The hope is that one could measure body fluids, neurotransmitters, behavioral indicators and the like, to see who will most likely be an addict. The logic states that if we can predetermine the identity of the ten percent of the general population that is at-risk to develop addiction, we could warn them. We also could aim early intervention and prevention-education programs at them.

The concept has possibilities, but consider that the marijuana growers of America, or the cocaine cartel, would also be supporters of the quest for the test. If one thousand people were to be screened with the "test," probably about ten percent, or one hundred people, would show up as predisposed and the remaining nine hundred people would not. Those nine hundred would get the message that they could base and drink all they wanted without risking addiction. It could be a license to be irresponsible.

What Are We Treating?

Addicts enter treatment because of events and behaviors involving harm to others. As a society we are understandably less concerned about the damaging effects of drugs on the individual drug user, how much psychoactive substance people ingest, than the pain and havoc this creates for other members of the community. Nevertheless, in the chemical dependency field, we commonly equate successful treatment with abstinence from drug use.

For example, consider the client who enters treatment because each time she smokes crack she goes home and abuses her young children. If she completes treatment and abstains from crack but still hurts her children, is her treatment a success? If she finishes treatment, smokes crack but never beats her children again, is her treatment a failure? What are we treating?

Compulsive use of psychoactive chemicals correlates with some bizarre behaviors, but abstinence from chemicals does not necessarily mean cessation of these behaviors. Treatment is a two-fold task of first teaching and counseling the client into a drug free lifestyle, and then teaching the client the skills to improve the quality of life. In treating crack cocaine addiction, we must teach the client how to be functional.

DENIAL

. . . Now They're Going to Lie to You

Counselors are often told from the first day of work in chemical dependency treatment that clients will lie and deny . . . especially crack addicts. I disagree. This assumption is destructive to the client, the counselor and the helping relationship. Denial is a sly accusation. Once a charge of denial has been leveled at someone, how can that person defend himself without confirming the suspicion, diagnosis, or allegation? This is the double-bind of the denial mind-set. Yes, addicts use denial, as do non-addicts. In my experience with crack addicts, I have found that they do not use denial as a defense mechanism any more often than does the general population.

Disguised as Denial

What counselors diagnose as denial often reveals only a lack of information about what is normal in the client's circumstances. I once interviewed a good old boy from Alabama, who came to see me after a threat from his wife. He told me he drank "alkeyhall," but was a normal drinker. In my counselor's wisdom, I asked him how much he drank per day. He responded, without batting an eye, "two six packs per day Dr. George." Who is this, I wondered, to think that drinking two six-packs per day is normal? He must be in denial. Instead of trying to break down this man's denial, like a well-conditioned (not well-trained) counselor, I asked, "How much beer do your drinking buddies drink?" Again, without batting an eye, he said, "Well, Dr. George, they're heavy drinkers. They drink three or four six-packs each day." He was not in denial. He did not know what normal was. In his frame of reference, two six-packs per day was moderate or normal use.

Sometimes counselors are quick to label clients simply because they don't answer the way we think they should. Often, we never consider that they lack information about what is normal drug or alcohol use. Beyond that, often counselors themselves don't know what is normal. How many counselors know the normal rate of alcohol consumption for an adult American? Most of us use our own frame of reference. If a client drinks more than I do, he drinks too much. If she drinks about the same amount, she's a normal drinker.

Consider this research on client denial. A treatment program staff was asked to divide the inpatient client population into two groups: clients high in denial and clients low in denial. The staff assembled to review their caseload. "Jim, oh yeh, he's definitely high in denial. Susie, nah, she's low in denial. George; man, he's super-high in denial!" The clinicians put together their list.

Next, independent researchers looked at the groups and noted the differences. The independent researchers did not know that denial was being studied. When the two groups were compared they found the group originally classified as high in denial was self-directed and assertive. The group classified as low in denial was passive, acquiescent and neurotic.[1]

People who were classified as low in denial, the clients we see as more motivated are actually the same clients whose traits, passivity and acquiescence, make them nonassertive. Who would adapt better after treatment, a person who is passive or a person who is self-directed and assertive? If you believe that recovery is based on surrender, who is more likely to benefit from surrender: a passive, acquiescent person or a self-directed, assertive person? Who is more likely to follow through independently with a continuing care plan or attend self-help meetings regularly? The answer is usually the self-directed person.

Denial is common in the addiction field, but it is more often a counselor fallacy than a client phenomenon. Some-

---

1. This research was cited in W.R. Miller, "Motivation for Treatment: A Review with Emphasis on Alcoholism," *Psychological Bulletin* 98, no.1(1985): 84-107. Current interest in denial can be seen in the shift in the field from conceptualizing denial within a psychodynamic model to more of a social model. See: D. Brissett, "Denial in Alcoholism: A Sociological Interpretation," *Journal of Drug Issues* 18, no.3(1988):385-402; R.E. Tarter, A.I. Alterman, and K.L. Edwards, "Alcoholic Denial: A Biopsychological Interpretation," *Journal of Studies on Alcohol* 45, no.3(1984): 214-218.

times counselors think, "If you agree with me you are low in denial, and if you disagree with me you are high in denial." That logic stems from the old medical adage, "If you get better it's because of me. If you stay sick, it's because of you. You're not motivated; you're too defensive; you're in denial!"

Resistance as a Survival Mechanism

Two crack addicts sat under the bridge taking hits off the glass stick. The skinnier one turned to his smoking buddy and said, "Hey old man, did you ever think about going to one of those treatment programs to get off the rocks?"

The old man took a big suck of vapors, leaned back, coughed up some black phlegm, wiped his mouth and spoke. "Let me tell you about my one try at that treatment stuff. But, first, I got to tell you about how I started drugging like this. I used to be a working person, used to wear a suit and tie to work. I had a regular nine-to-five job and made good money. I had a wife, a couple of kids even," he said with misty eyes. "One night, after work, a long time ago . . . seems like a million years ago now . . . I went out for a drink with a couple buddies. We had a few and you know what, we ended up buying some rocks . . . for the first time. That crack made me feel good. Real good. A few hits made me forget all the pressures at work. Well, I got home late and my wife started to nag at me. I really didn't want to hear it.

"The next night I went out with my buddies again. Well, you know the story. I started getting into the stuff and letting other things slide. I'd get home from the bar late. My wife would be angry and disappointed with me. But, you know, I didn't care because the pipe and the feelings I got from it helped me forget my wife's nagging. Well, I started avoiding my kids. I didn't want to be around them when I was smoking because I really wasn't being much of a dad anyway. The pipe was more important to me than the kids, after a while. And the job, well, you know I lost that. I couldn't get up each morning and get to work when I was crashing and feeling sick. The pipe got to be more important to me than my job, or my kids or my wife. After a while, I lost them all. But I still had the pipe. That's all I had left; everything else was gone.

"Finally, I found myself sitting on the floor in a crack house with a three-day growth of beard on my face. I had no wife, no kids, no family, no job. I lost them all for the pipe, and all I had left with me was that pipe. I looked across the street, you know, out the window, and saw that treatment program. It was that one that's always advertising on TV. I walked in the door and told them I needed help. They asked me for my insurance card. Can you believe it? When I told them I didn't have one, they sent me to the public program across town. Well, I walked 15 blocks to get there. I walked in the door, carrying my pipe and what was my last crumbs. I was feeling bad, real bad.

"This young kid came up to me. He asked me if I wanted help. 'Sure . . . why else would I be here,' I told him. He said he was going to take my pipe from me. I pulled back right away and told him that he wasn't going to take that pipe from me. I told him it was all I had left in my life. I told him that my pipe wasn't just a pipe—it was my wife, my kids, my job. It was what I gave up all those important things in my life for. It wasn't just a pipe. It was all I had left. This crack pipe was worth losing the love of my wife. This pipe was worth losing the respect and pride from my kids, the trust in my kids' faces when they looked at their daddy. This pipe was worth the loss of my job and my work friends. 'No,' I told that young counselor, 'I'm not gonna give you my pipe. That's all I have left in my life. Please don't take this too.'

"You know what that counselor said to me? He told me I wasn't motivated to change my life, that I was in denial about my drugging and that I was resistent to treatment. He told me to come back when I could appreciate what he was trying to do for me and was willing to give up my pipe.

"I guess I didn't have that motivation then. I guess I was resistant to change. But, I haven't changed a whole lot since then. I'm still not handing over this pipe to a stranger. I guess I'm not ready to stop yet.

"Sometimes I wish that young counselor had understood what that pipe meant to me. Maybe if he would have told me that if I gave him the pipe he'd give me back my family, my job, my wife, my kids, or if not those things, maybe he could have told me if I gave him the pipe he'd give me back some self-respect and dignity. At least that would have been some kind of a trade. To give up all I had for nothing? No, I couldn't do that then and I couldn't do that now. I guess I am resistant to change. Maybe tomorrow, maybe tomorrow. Now, how about another hit on that?"

To test the validity of your judgment concerning denial, try this experiment. Assume addicts do not use denial any more than anyone else. Do not look for evidence of denial. See if you become entangled in as many problems related to breaking down the denial. While working with the assumption that addicts use denial no more than the rest of us, do another experiment. Make up a ridiculous symptom of addiction . . . eye blinking, foot tapping, or nose scratching. Tell yourself it is a major symptom of addiction. It's a good bet you'll see addicts doing that behavior frequently over the next few months. You will have sensitized yourself to something insignificant. The same sensitization can occur when we constantly discuss client denial and all its horrendous implications.

What about lying? There is a widespread belief among chemical dependency counselors that crack addicts are habitual liars. This has serious consequences for the counselor-client interaction. I challenge anyone to enter a relationship with another human being, while assuming that they will lie, and to develop a productive, meaningful relationship.

It has been my experience as a counselor of crack addicts that if you ask the right questions in the right atmosphere, clients give valid answers. We, as counselors, sometimes fail to follow this simple rule and receive answers to our questions that seem to be lies. As in the earlier example, we might ask clients how much alcohol they use. They understate it. Perhaps this understatement of fact isn't a lie but a consequence of the client not considering beer to be alcohol. We ask about drug use, and a client fails to mention marijuana or prescription medications. Many young people still don't consider marijuana a drug. For some abusers, it's a benign staple of everyday life. Clients often don't consider prescription medications to be drugs, so they exclude them in response to general questions about drug use. If you ask specific questions about drug use you generally get valid information. Ask about the frequency, intensity, and duration of use. Ask how often they smoke marijuana; how often they use beer, wine coolers, mixed drinks; how often they take prescription medications, over-the-counter medications.

An Atmosphere for Self-Disclosure

The degree of self-disclosure by any individual is directly proportional to the level of pain they experience at that moment or to the trust they have in the person with whom they are speaking. Typically, clients are already in pain when you see them. The counselor's mission is to create an atmosphere of trust. We cannot expect crack addicts who are crashing from the drug and feeling paranoid to respond well to questions about illicit drug use when interviewed in a public setting or in a situation that reminds them of the man, the police. Don't expect crack addicts to self-disclose valid information after you inform them that all the information will be sent to their probation officer. We must make a serious effort to minimize any "secondary gain" the client might get from lying.

It is a good idea for counselors to throw out the word *lying* and reframe it with the word *inconsistencies*. If a crack addict gives conflicting data, point out inconsistencies. Do not imply that the client lied. It is easier to hear that we have been inconsistent than to be called a liar. Anyone would feel less defensive if confronted in that manner.

Confrontation: Constructive or Destructive?

Confrontation is another important issue for crack counselors. I began working in the old therapeutic community days when confrontation was different and less productive than the techniques I now use with crack addicts. We confronted people in groups when we were angry or frustrated with them, or when we didn't know what else to do. Our confrontation went like this: "Hey, you shithead, get it together." Bad feedback! That method is not focused, specific, or aimed at a changeable behavior. It is not confrontation; it is rude, irresponsible and unproductive.

If you confront me that way, embarrass and humiliate me in public, or show disrespect for me, I will change my behaviors . . . around you. If you rudely confront me over my anger or violence, I may become passive and compliant around you. But when I leave, I'll go home and yell at my wife and beat the cat or the kids! I'll remember all those things you belittled and do them when you aren't around. I'll learn a lesson from you. I'll learn I can't be who I am around you and to stuff my behaviors around you. I'll learn that your regard is conditional. I'll learn to act compliant, acquiescent and passive. If I'm a good sociopath or a person socialized by the street, I may even learn to model your rudeness to gain power over other passive members, especially other frail, broken spirits. Most counselors have seen this with older, broken down gamma alcoholics who are in group sessions with a few streetwise crack addicts. If someone models the attacking form of confrontation, the crack addicts, well-trained in survival, use that tool to run roughshod over the less aggressive alcoholics.

Programs that operate from this destructive model of confrontation involve staff who pride themselves in their ability to tear down denial, resistance, and to gain control. They're delusional if they think they are that powerful. Those programs usually have high Against Medical Advice termination rates. They explain this by claiming that clients weren't ready to work. Those programs create clients who are compliant drones, shuffling through the moves and never accomplishing anything significant. Those programs have taught clients well, to be obedient and to stuff what is real. Those programs have taught clients not to feel, trust or talk. They have taken over where the streets and dysfunctional family legacies ended, carrying on the heritage of dysfunction. Their clients self-destruct in out-of-control relapse the day they leave treatment because the clients really haven't been taught anything new. They were reinforced to act controlling, manipulative, and antireal, not just antisocial.

Confrontation should not be an attack. Confrontation means pointing out to clients where they say they want to be in their life and where they now are. It means focusing on the discrepancy.

Confrontation, like feedback, needs to be descriptive and not evaluative. It needs to be specific and not general, aimed at a changeable behavior. It works best if solicited, not dumped. It should be owned by the giver, and not presented as universal truth. It needs to be well-timed.

Confrontation is a wonderful, powerful tool for clinical use. When used appropriately, as feedback, it may be the most powerful change agent available. It is our responsibility as counselors to learn how to use it correctly.

Motivation: Verbal or Behavioral Compliance?

Susan entered the staff lounge obviously enraged at the world. "These damn clients are really pissing me off," she shouted, "especially that new guy, Jim. You know, he's that crack addict who's been here for three weeks. He just sat on his ass in group and told them he's here only because he's sick of the streets and wanted a vacation. He told us of his plans 'to use' as soon as he gets out of treatment in three more weeks. He said the group therapy here is a bunch of bullshit. I'm ready to kick him out of treatment. We should send him out now because he is still in denial and lacks motivation to change. I think we should discharge him. We need room for people who really want to get their lives together. Besides all that, he told the group that he's going to stiff us on the bill for treatment. He only paid half down before admission, and he doesn't have any health insurance. He threatened to burn us on the other $5000 he owes for the next three weeks."

Karen, another counselor, looked at Susan with compassion. "Susan, let me get this clear. Jim has been in treatment for three weeks so far, right? He attended all group sessions to date, right? He has paid $5000 out of his pocket for treatment so far, right? He opened up in group today and expressing feeling, right? He's being assertive in group, right? He stated that he will be with us for three more weeks, right?" Susan nodded. "And," continued Karen, "it's group time right now. By the way, are the clients on break or what?" "No," responded Susan, "I was so pissed off I walked out of group. They're still in there doing something." "Seems to me," Karen reflected, "that we do have a problem in our program with some people lacking motivation, but, I don't believe it's Jim."

No one volunteers for treatment. I first learned this in a group therapy session when a client stood up and shouted, "I'm not like you, Kim. The courts made you come into treatment. I'm not like you, John. Your boss told you to get treatment or he'd fire your ass. I'm sure not like you, Alan. Your wife pushed you to be here. I'm different. I wasn't forced into treatment. I volunteered." This volunteer came for help after he lost his wife, his children, his job, his house, his car and his dignity. People tend to change when their feet are stuck in the fire, and they have few, if any, alternatives.

II

Crack: The Treatment

CONTACT

Empowering The Counselor

Your first contact with a crack addicted client probably
will be by telephone. Chances are the call will come from
one of several sources: a professional referral, a criminal
justice referral, a family member or sometimes, although
infrequently, the crack addict himself will seek help.
Maximizing your effectiveness as a counselor begins with
this initial contact.

Referrals by other professionals or from the criminal
justice system usually do not require careful finessing or
"hooking" of the client. Crack addicts referred by these
sources will generally appear for the first session, the
initial assessment. When a family member calls about a
relative's addiction or when the troubled client calls, you
will often have to use techniques to remove obstacles and
to minimize resistance to treatment. Getting into treatment should be made easy for the crack addict. Let's look
at some techniques to promote this.

Empower Yourself

If a member of a crack addict's family calls you to ask about treatment, empower yourself. It is almost certain that the person calling has tried, and failed, to correct the problem, to get the relative to stop smoking rocks and to cease bizarre behaviors. Home methods haven't worked; otherwise the family member wouldn't be calling a stranger for help.

Take advantage of this. Let the caller know by the way you handle the call that you are an expert in crack cocaine addiction and chemical dependency treatment. No one wants to follow the recommendations of a professional who appears insecure or uncertain about what to do or recommend. Empower yourself by using your knowledge to hook the person into treatment. This idea of counselor empowerment will be familiar to readers who are trained in family therapy. Successful family therapists are masters of establishing credibility with their clients.

When family members call, they will undoubtedly tell you a story about their plight, a story you will have heard many times before. From your experience as a chemical dependency counselor you can predict what a caller has been through and that caller's feelings. Let callers know you understand what they are going through. Reassure them that their attempts at intervention are admirable, despite their ineffectiveness, and that their reactions to the problem of crack addiction are normal. Verbalize their feelings, and also reassure them that it is normal to experience these feelings. Find out as much as you can about the family, those involved with the problem and how they interact with the addict. Use your knowledge of family dynamics to convince the caller you understand the family's dilemma.

By using your ability to understand first-time callers, reflecting back to them how they feel, how they react to the crack addict in their family, and what they have probably tried to do in the past, you empower yourself as a competent, credible counselor who can help them. You also provide an anchor for someone who needs a stable force at that exact moment in life. It is a win-win situation. You have more influence over the caller because of your obvious professional knowledge and competency. The caller feels his sanity is confirmed, and receives some positive reinforcement for having picked up the phone and called for help.

A Clinical Scenario

The following is an illustration of how an early encounter evolves.

The phone on your desk rings. You pick it up and hear a woman say,

Hello, I'm calling for my husband, who is smoking crack. I've tried everything to get him to stop, but he still smokes. Our family is falling apart.

Based on what you heard in this first brief message, what do you now know about the caller? She has a family. She is frustrated and worried about it. Her husband smokes rocks and is causing family problems. She tried unsuccessfully to get him to stop, but she is still committed to helping him.

We can assume that she has the same feelings that other spouses of crack addicts have expressed. She is angry, resentful, guilty and blames herself for his drug use. Having taken on the responsibilities of the family herself, she feels under intense pressure. She may have tried to base or drink with him to pace him at the crack house or bar. She may have gone hit-for-hit or drink for drink to slow him down, and is beginning to develop a drug problem herself. She may be on medications for stress-related problems associated with her role in the family. She may have somatic complaints. She may have tried the usual things spouses do: dumping the crack down the toilet, yelling at the addict when he spends more on another eight ball. She probably is hiding money and valuable family belongings from the addict. She may have tried to be a super spouse, to do everything perfectly and to eliminate all the pressure and stress in the crack addict's life. Finally, in desperation, she may have threatened to leave with the children unless he stops, but has not followed through on the threat.

We can predict that the family follows the typical pattern of families of chemically dependent persons. We can speculate about the roles and rules of each family member. We can predict how each child will act based upon what we know about the dynamics of addictive family systems. In responding to the caller, we use some of our knowledge of crack addiction and family dynamics to establish a strong and positive professional relationship. A counselor, for example, could respond as described below.

An Empowering Response

You sound really frustrated and hurt over your husband's crack smoking. I bet you've begun to ask yourself if you are to blame. Some spouses go so far as believing they can cure their spouse by themselves. I'm glad you don't believe that. You wouldn't have called a professional for help if you did. In my years of experience with cocaine addiction, I have learned what you know, that you can't do it all yourself. Come in at four o'clock this afternoon and let's share some strategies. We will come up with Plan A. It works most of the time. If, for some reason, it doesn't, there's always Plan B. Now, please give me your phone number and permission to call you back, just in case something comes up and you can't make it at four today. I don't want to lose you.

It is important to remember that whoever calls you for help is a person in a crisis. Although the caller may not be the crack addict, the caller does need some accommodation, structure and support. The illustrative response will ease the mind of someone in a crisis.

Crack: The Treatment

When An Addict Calls

Next, consider a case that begins with a call from the crack addict. The first thing to remember is that crack addicts typically do not volunteer to go into treatment because it's a good idea or because they want to improve themselves. The motivation to pick up the phone to get help comes from either a critical event (a DUI, public embarrassment, or violating some personal value such as beating a spouse or child) or a series of minor crisis events that build up to a phone call for help. The person calling may be sober or intoxicated. When I speak to an addict calling for help, I usually assume he is under the influence.

Counselors should empower themselves with the crack addict, just as with the family member who calls. The approach is somewhat different. Whereas some methods will work to help you engage a family member, the same methods may not work as well with the crack addict.

It is more appropriate to disclose your history of addiction if the caller is a crack addict than if the caller is an addict's family member. This could be a red flag for a family member, but it probably will be a good technique for establishing rapport with the crack addict. Any self-disclosure should focus on the addictive process and recovery, not the personal aspects of your story. The message you want to convey to the caller is that you understand. You have been there, and recovery is possible. Treatment can work.

It is advisable to have the caller write down important information as you give it. This includes simple things such as your name, your organization, your telephone number, the date and time the crack addict is to come in for an assessment and any other specific instructions, such as "Go to detox at 111 West X Street now."

This may sound foolish. Callers already know your telephone number. Still, an addict who calls may be in a blackout. I go even farther than this when I speak to active addicts calling for help. I ask them to write down some exact sentences they used, such as, "I'm sick of this and I need some help" or "I'll do anything I need to do to get better." Sometimes that written record of their statements gives them the boost they need to get off the phone and come in for treatment.

Give specific, concrete instructions to any caller who is seeking services. They need direction now. There is a limited window of opportunity. If you miss it or delay it due to your clinic's inability to respond quickly and accommodate, you may deny the caller a last chance for sobriety. You do not want the call for help to go down in the caller's memory as another dead end, another failure.

FAMILY INVOLVEMENT

Interrupting the Flow of Events

If you did a great job of hooking the crack addict or family member into coming in for an initial session, you now face the task of convincing the addict to enter treatment if, based on your assessment, it is needed. The technique of raising the bottom, helps addicts see clearly the need for professional help. It is a process called "intervention." Intervention is an interruption of the normal flow of events in an addict's life through actions consciously designed to persuade the addict that now is the time to enter treatment. Successful interventions slow or stop the addictive progression, but poor interventions tend to accelerate it.

Guidelines for Intervention

Since the early 1980s, chemical dependency intervention has usually been based on the Johnson Institute model, a systematic, step-by-step method for getting help for addicts who are reluctant to help themselves.[1] It works well. There are other approaches to intervention that have proven effective. Some of these are less structured and less time consuming. In reviewing intervention models, I have identified eleven crucial guidelines that should be followed with the crack addict. I discuss these guidelines with clients who consult me when a loved one is drugging. Father Martin, a leading expert on addictions, says that each human has the power to save another human's life. These eleven guidelines may do this by getting the crack addict in to see a professional before it's too late.

Guideline 1. Don't waste your time talking about a serious drug problem with someone who is high.

For professionals, this is self-explanatory. For the general population it is not. Every day I hear from people who have confronted their loved ones about drinking and drugging when the users are so high it is impossible to carry on a rational conversation. Even if, for some miraculous reason, they can carry on a conversation that approaches normalcy, the addicts may be in a blackout and not remember anything that was said. When I speak about Guideline 1, I inform clients that, normally, family members only talk to addicts about their drug problem when the addict is high. That is when family members and

---

1. Much of the material on interventions has evolved from the works of Vern Johnson. See Vern E. Johnson, *Intervention: How to Help Someone Who Doesn't Want Help* (Minneapolis: Johnson Institute Books, 1986).

friends are so angry that they are willing to take the risk. Unfortunately, it doesn't help.

Guideline 2. Speak to addicts about their drug problem in the morning, before they have a chance to get high or defensive.

Crack addicts are like the rest of us. They are least defensive when they wake up. As the day progresses, life builds walls. If you can catch the addict in the morning, especially on a Saturday or Sunday morning after a night of drugging and drinking, the addict will be more open to what you have to say. This is the window of opportunity.

Guideline 3. Express care and concern for the crack addict.

Do not discuss the drug problem when you are angry, extremely resentful or too emotional. Crack addicts respond best when seduced, not beaten, into treatment. Addicts can sense if you are hateful, disgusted with them or spiteful. Would you take the advice of an adversary? Wait until you have your feet on the ground before you intervene.

Guideline 4. If you confront an addict with a problem (drugging), always offer a solution.

To confront an addict about substance abuse without offering a way out is nothing more than criticism, whatever your intent. This will only increase the crack addict's defensiveness.

Guideline 5. Talk about behaviors you yourself have seen, not things you hear secondhand.

Tell the addict how the behavior made you feel. Ask him to get help. This is absolutely essential in the intervention process. When you talk to the crack addict, speak in behavioral terms about real events. Share with the addict the feelings you had when certain behaviors were displayed.

A good example comes from an intervention in which I was involved. The client was an eighty-six-year-old man who was extremely stubborn. Nothing his family said had any impact on him. He was determined to continue his drinking and drugging until he died. Finally, his seven-year-old great-granddaughter spoke.

"Pappa," she said, "two weeks ago I had my first piano recital at school. When you came in you knocked over a chair. You smelled bad. I was embarrassed. I want you to hear me play the piano, but I don't want to feel like that again."

Pappa entered treatment.

Recommend that family and friends use the feedback model. Ask the family to recall examples of specific behaviors and write them into the feedback model format:

Feedback Model Format

(specific time) when you (specific behavior), I felt (specific feeling) and wanted to (specific behavior). Please get some help from (specific person and time).

A completed example of the feedback format is:

"Last thursday when you *arrived four hours late for dinner,* I felt *angry, disappointed and hurt,* and wanted to *throw you out the door.* Please get some help from *Dr. Smith next tuesday, I have set up an appointment for 4 PM."*

Guideline 6. Offer the crack addict support.

Offer to go along to the initial appointment. Offer to sit in the waiting room during counseling if the crack addict is afraid. Offer to sit next to him and hold his hand during the interview. Communicate a sense of support.

Guideline 7. Let the crack addict know that you're only asking for an initial one-hour appointment, to speak and listen to an expert in the field.

Nobody wants to give up a habit. If you even imply, during the initial session, that your expectation is lifelong sobriety, the crack addict will tell you, either verbally or nonverbally, "I'm out of here!" Reassure your client that he does not have to make a lifelong promise to stop drugging and drinking and that he does not have to enter a program immediately. He only needs to see an expert and discuss his life for one hour, with an open mind.

Guideline 8. If the crack addict still refuses to see a professional for an initial session, ask him to do it *for you*.

Some might say that it is behaving like a codependent to ask an addict to get help for you. Caring is not codependency. People do owe their friends something. It is the other side of the equation of a relationship. Tell your addicted friend to do it for you, even if he doesn't want to do it for himself. He owes you at least one hour out of his life, an hour that may save it.

Relationship pressure and social obligations do indeed influence addicts. They are not completely self-absorbed. For example, in a treatment program in Kathmandu, Nepal, a family came in for an intervention. There before me on the floor sat a 21-year-old heroin addict in withdrawal. Next to him was his older brother, about 25 years old. Next was Mom and Dad. Completing the circle was the counselor, a Jesuit priest who ran the program.

The intervention took place in Nepali, the local language. I could follow most of what was going on since family and group dynamics are not culturally unique. After some interactions, the young heroin addict agreed to enter treatment.

Then, something happened. The priest began speaking directly to the father. It seemed the priest was doing an intervention on the dad, who I learned later was an alcoholic. The priest kept speaking, but the father kept shaking his head. Finally, after close to twenty minutes, the father agreed to treatment for himself.

Later, when the priest and I debriefed the session, I asked him how he got the father to enter treatment. He told me that in Nepali there is a word for wise old man. He said, "It is a sign of respect. The word is Bagee (or grandfather). I told this man, a Bagee, that you were a doctor from a far away land. I told him he and I are both Bagees, and that he had disrespected me, a fellow Bagee, in front of a foreigner. The father was so ashamed for disrespecting me that he agreed to treatment to let me save face in front of you, George."

Guideline 9. Make sure you have an appointment set up before you confront the crack addict.

Crack addicts tend to be impulsive and impatient. If they decide to see someone for help, they don't want to wait a few days or hours. If you have an appointment already made, there is a better chance they will follow through.

Guideline 10. If the crack addict still refuses an appointment, don't give up; try Plan B.

Plan B may be a formal Johnson Institute Intervention, or it may be a legal intervention in the form of commitment. Court-ordered treatment can work as well as so-called voluntary treatment. Research results confirm this.[2] Usually it isn't necessary to go the legal route to initiate an involuntary treatment order. With the intervention models available, the family has alternatives to involuntary court orders for the treatment of loved ones. Although most states have mechanisms for court-ordered treatment, most families prefer to use an intervention, as opposed to legal methods. The outcome for voluntary and involuntary referrals may be the same, but voluntary referrals, initiated by intervention, often are gentler on the family members.

Guideline 11. No matter what the outcome with the crack addict, family members should be encouraged to obtain family counseling or to participate in community self-help groups.

Intervention, whether successful or unsuccessful, is only one side of the treatment equation. It is designed to help the crack addict, and, only to a limited extent, the family. When families and friends of crack addicts consult with me about interventions, I stress that an intervention will help them learn how to talk to an addict about a problem. But they must "pay" me for the help by going to Alanon, Naranon or other community support groups. Often, involvement in these self-help groups is sufficient to establish the family on a better footing when the crack addict begins

---

2. There is an expanding quantity of information on motivation, and voluntary vs. involuntary treatment. W. R. Miller presents an excellent review of the literature. See W.R. Miller, "Motivation for Treatment: A Review with Special Emphasis on Alcoholism," *Psychological Bulletin* 98,no.1 (1985):84-107.

treatment. In other cases, the life of the family has been so adversely affected by the crack addiction that family therapy is required.

Family Therapy

Family therapy is the art and science of developing inclusion, control, and affection between members of the family system, elements which often have been destroyed or disrupted by the addiction.[3] In conducting therapy with members of the crack addict's family, the counselor assesses what is broken within the family, and determines how it can be fixed by changing: (1) *the boundaries,* the distance between each member; (2) *the subsystems*, the groups of family members who are in charge of roles and rules, parenting, and being parented; (3) *interaction patterns*, lines of communication of thoughts and emotions between and among each member within the family structure.[4]

Family therapy is a prescriptive, proactive and technically difficult method of treatment. Effective delivery of family therapy requires that the counselor receive special-

---

3. The concepts of inclusion, control and affection can be found in William C. Schutz, *The Interpersonal Underworld* (Palo Alto: Science and Behavior Books, 1966), 13-33. I think these concepts strongly support the need to empower rather than disempower clients in treatment.

4. S. Minuchen, *Families and Family Therapy* (Cambridge, Mass.: Harvard University Press, 1974).

ized training. The following is a brief overview of some of the aspects of family therapy which apply to chemical dependency counseling with crack addicts.[5]

Boundaries and the concept of *inclusion* are closely related. The more rigid the boundaries between family members, the greater the distance between them and the weaker the feelings of belonging or inclusion. The more diffused, or thin, the boundaries are between members, the more included they tend to be. Consider the differences between two family structures. One has rigid boundaries, walls between each member of the family system. As a result, a commom problem of this type of family is weak feelings of belonging or inclusion, a lack of family identity. The other family has thin or diffused boundaries and, consequently, a better sense of family identity or inclusion, but individual members may have difficulty in separating and developing the independence of adulthood.

For the family with rigid, strong boundaries between individuals, the therapist may need to diffuse, or thin down, those boundaries. Families whose members are too distant from one another need to be helped to weaken their boundaries, in order to promote feelings of belonging

---

5. Several good references on family therapy, in general, and family therapy with the addict, are: S. Wegsheider, *Another Chance - Hope and Health for the Alcoholic* (Palo Alto: Science and Behavior Books, 1981); M.D. Stanton and T.C.Todd, T.C., *The Family Therapy of Drug Abuse and Addiction* (New York: The Guilford Press, 1982).

and of family identity. There should be, for example, a lot of glue, or closeness, between parents and young children to permit the development of bonding and the establishment of feelings of trust and safety.

On the other hand, in families where boundaries between individual members are too thin, family members may be too close and may need to have more distance. The therapist, then, needs to strengthen the boundaries, to create greater distance between individuals, to promote the development of independence, particularly for teenagers and young adults.

Subsystems, as explained by structural family therapists, are the executive, parental, and sibling. The executive subsystem in a typical family consists of the mother and father, although in extended families it may include others, such as grandparents. The executive subsystem is the top of the family's power structure, responsible for establishing rules, norms, and mores for the entire family. They pass along the family traditions, too. Members of the executive subsystem provide structure for the family by establishing "bylaws."

The parental subsystem is the unit responsible for rearing the children. It establishes the rules for how children will operate within the family, and orients them to those rules so everyone knows how to act right. The mother and father are typically the parental subsystem, although, in extended families, grandparents may be included.

The sibling subsystem's job is to foster compliance with the laws of the family as set forth by the executive subsystem, and the rules for being children within that specific family, as set forth by the parental subsystem. Siblings must play their role well if the parental and executive subsystems are to function effectively because there is a degree of interdependence among the three subsystems. Each has some power over the other. If one of the subsystems does not perform as assigned, the others cannot either. This is the control function of the family.

In families with an addicted member, the subsystems become unbalanced, distorted, and in need of modification. Often parents act like children, becoming part of the sibling subsystem; children act like parents, assuming control of the parental subsystem; and nobody follows a fixed set of rules. Continuing conflicts over who represents the executive subsystem ebb and flow with the changing moods of family members. Sometimes a therapist can adjust these subsystems by making family members intellectually aware of how they function and by empowering of certain targeted members. For example, a therapist strengthens the parents as parental subsystem members by always referring to them as Mr. and Ms., while using first names with their children.

Interaction patterns are the conduits through which communications flow. They may be constricted, with little room for words, feelings, and thoughts to travel, or broad and flexible, with great capacity. If these conduits are blocked, emotions back up. Families with poor interaction patterns usually have no way of flushing out the feelings and emotions which continually well up. When the interactional patterns are free-flowing in both directions, there is a mutually beneficial exchange of words, thoughts, and feelings.

Interaction patterns may need to be strengthened or weakened. Perhaps communications are poor between a father and his young son. In this situation a counselor might prescribe that they go fishing together one day per week. If there are diffused boundaries between members to the point that when one has a headache the other takes an aspirin, the counselor might attempt to disengage them by structuring time away from each other. This will pull them apart to normal limits. If a counselor sees that a husband and wife rely on each other exclusively for emotional interaction, a weekly independent activity outside the home might be prescribed. This is what is routinely done with spouses of crack addicts. Some call these spouses codependents.

Codependency means that there is too much glue in a relationship, that the interaction is too strong. In response to this, counselors often prescribe that the codependent go to Alanon or CoDep meetings two of three times per week to learn about their codependent nature. When the spouses find themselves becoming less codependent, after attending meetings for several weeks, some counselors misinterpret this to mean that the codependent is making progress with the "disease." I believe this is not always the case.

Crack: The Treatment

Codependency describes an interaction pattern. It is not a psychodiagnostic category. A more direct explanation of the recovery is that the codependent is getting better simply by being away from the crack addict three nights per week and meeting other people. Freedom from interacting with the addict is watering down the glue. They are disengaging. It may be that if the codependent went bowling three nights per week, the codependency pattern would abate just as quickly. In fact, it might be more healthy because negative self-statements wouldn't be reinforced. The codependent wouldn't be required to self-disclose, three hours a week in public, how sick he is to a group of other people who are also convinced that they are sick. It is unfortunate that in our culture, the accepted forum to share personal feelings, problems, or life challenges with others is frequently limited to therapy or self-help groups. In other cultures and countries, I have noted that much of this is accomplished through personal friendships or through religious institutions.

There is no "normal" family, but developmental psychology provides guidelines for understanding what behaviors are standard for people of different ages. Counselors need to adjust this developmental model for individual families by considering factors such as nationality, race, and subculture, to mention a few. It is important for counseling, as a field, to break away from simplistic thinking. There is no test to see if a family is functional or dysfunctional based on twenty questions. There are too many confounding variables.

This also applies to the concept of how addicted families function. The film *Family Trap* is truly a great film, a staple in the treatment community, that has opened the eyes of millions of people to the impact of chemical dependency on the entire family system. In the film, Sharon Wegscheider-Cruse conveys concepts surrounding the roles and rules common in high-stress or addicted systems.[6] Unfortunately, too many people who see it (counselors included) think the various categories of family members—the Chemically Dependent, the Enabler, Hero, Scapegoat, Lost Child, and Pet—presented in the film are a firm standard. This is not true. The film shows clearly that change within one member triggers changes within others. It should not be interpreted as meaning that all addicted families function in the exact manner presented in the film.

Counselors should be aware that cultural factors also influence the nature and results of our assessments. There are many checklists available to counselors which purportedly pinpoint whether a client is an addict, a codependent, or suffering from ACOA syndrome. However, when interpreting results from these checklists a counselor must be sure that differences in social class, age, race, nationality, and cultures are not influencing the assessment. Consider this hypothetical checklist for codependency:

---

6. Readers may also want to review: Sharon Wegscheider, *Another Chance - Hope and Health for the Alcoholic* (Palo Alto: Science and Behavior Books, 1981).

1. I constantly compromise my personal goals for others.

2. I let the needs of others outweigh my own needs.

3. I feel my life is secondary to others.

4. I often change my plans to please others.

5. Sometimes I feel disappointed when I cannot do what I want to do because of others' needs.

This questionnaire seems to have face validity for assessing codependency. If it were given to Mother Teresa, she would rate as an extremely dysfunctional codependent. Give this codependency questionnaire to a single mother of three children ages one, two, and three, and you will find another codependent. There is no standard to measure where enmeshment becomes dysfunctional. The diagnosis is subjective.

What are the best environments for family counseling? A group format usually works better than individual family therapy sessions but it is often necessary to begin with separate family sessions before moving a family into multi-family groups. While the family is in individual counseling, undertake the activities that work best in that format: joining with the family and establishing trust, collecting data and goal setting/treatment planning, crisis intervening, motivating the client toward group, behavioral contracting for early intervention, and specific skill-building.

A Caution

There is a natural temptation to shape the families we counsel like our own families of origin. This can be dangerous. Chemical dependency counseling is over-represented by recovering persons and children from alcoholic or drug dependent families. Some of the people who enter the helping professions have had serious family problems other than addiction. As counselors, we should thoroughly evaluate our own backgrounds and be careful that what we do and advocate is not a reflection from a distant mirror.

ASSESSMENT

Getting the Facts

A counselor's first clinical contact with the crack addict is focused on assessment and screening. Information obtained during this in-depth interview helps pinpoint the client's recovery needs and the methods and modalities that will be used in treatment. The important point for the counselor to remember is to collect as much *specific* data as possible. The more one can focus on specifics now, the more likely it is that planning, and the subsequent treatment program, will be effective.

Establishing Rapport

Studies show that the nature and quality of a counselor's first contact with a client has great impact on the client's general success in treatment. If counseling is viewed as a relationship between a professional and a client, as teamwork, there are better outcomes. A University of New Mexico study examined alcohol-use assessments, sessions where people could see if their drinking was at a problem level.[1] Clients were interviewed and data was collected by counselors. In this experiment, one-half of the counselors reported the results of the assessment to the clients in a nondirective, person-centered therapy format. After discussing the results, they recommended treatment, if it was warranted. The other counselors approached the clients authoritatively, stressing only the necessity of immediate treatment. If clients showed any disagreement or questioned the findings, the counselor attempted to persuade the client through direct confrontation. Then the "person-centered approach" and "direct confrontational" approaches were compared. Analysis of videotaped sessions showed less evidence of client resistance and denial with the person-centered approach.

It is essential to establish good rapport during the initial assessment session. The following is an example of an effective rapport-building technique. This illustration is based on a session involving family members, but the same technique could be used in a one-to-one assessment session with an addict.

Hello, . . . My name is Dr. George Medzerian. Please feel free to call me George, Dr. George, or Dr. Medzerian, whichever is more comfortable for you. I am a licensed psychologist with more than 17 years in

---

1. W. R. Miller and V. C. Sanchez. "Motivating Young Adults for Treatment and Lifestyle Change"Issues in Alcohol Use and Misuse by Young Adults." Paper presented at a conference at Notre Dame University, South Bend, Indiana, April 25-26, 1988.

the drug and alcohol treatment field. I want to thank you for coming here today. I know it's difficult to speak to a stranger about your problems, so I really admire your courage in coming in. My goal for today is to spend about an hour with you talking about what is going on in your life that I can help you with. After the hour I'll give you recommendations for further help if, in my professional opinion, you need any. The information you share will be confidential.

During the next hour you may have feelings or thoughts that are uncomfortable. This is normal. You may even feel embarrassed sharing some information with me or in front of your (family member) companion. Any time you feel like you're censoring information because of the person with you, please give me a signal. Raise your finger, so I'll know what's going on. Then one of you will go in the other room for a few minutes while we talk privately. Can we agree to this?

In an assessment session involving family members, most clients will agree to let you know if the session is too intense, and if they need private time with you. It's important to notice any signs of discomfort. The purpose of the assessment is to collect valid data; feelings of discomfort can inhibit addicts from revealing the truth about their problem. Even if no one signals they want some private communication, if you sense a growing discomfort, intervene and ask for a few moments of privacy with the person appearing uncomfortable. This won't be a shock to anyone because of your earlier statement.

105

Counselors also should let clients know that it is normal to experience intense feelings, to feel embarrassed and to want a loved one to leave the room so you can talk more freely. This process is sometimes called "norm setting." Norm setting should also reinforce the idea that this is a confidential interview and that the interviewer is experienced and well-trained.

When you join with the client or client's family during the initial assessment, you want them to be able to quickly know and trust you. Do this by sharing common activities, engaging the client and his family socially.

. . . Where are you folks from? Are you native Floridians or transplants? Oh, you used to live up north. Me too. I moved here about ten years ago.

. . . What do you do for a living? You know, I was in the Navy too about twenty years ago . . . it sure doesn't seem like that long ago though.

. . . Oh, you decided to move here after retiring from the Navy so you can enjoy the sports here. Are you a beach person or a sportsman? Yeh, me too. I love the beaches, and I do some fishing but I never tried fresh water fishing. Maybe you can give me some tips on good places to go for bass.

. . . You have any kids? Boy, they sure can keep your hands full, can't they!

This gives clients a quick sense of who you are: a northerner (just like them), an ex-navy person (just like them), a sports enthusiast (just like them). When you do this, clients will begin to feel comfortable, to think they know you because you both have common activities, interests and backgrounds.

It's small talk and it may sound hokey, but that's how relationships get started. People need to develop trust, which is the ability to predict with some degree of accuracy what a person will do under a certain set of circumstances. The spouses of addicts distrust crack addicts because they are so unpredictable. People regain trust when another person behaves consistently and predictably. Some professionals say that about one-sixth of therapy sessions should be spent with joining activities, or small talk. This equates to ten minutes per hour of therapy!

Shifting to Substantive Issues

Once you have spent part of the initial assessment session on these process/maintenance issues, shift emphasis to substantive issues. Your main assessment goal is to collect data about the addict's drug history and to evaluate this data using your knowledge of abuse and addiction, treatment methods and modalities. This will be filtered through your philosophy of treatment in order to make a recommendation for any needed services. Today's prevalent philosophy of treatment is to recommend the least restrictive treatment environment you judge will be effective for the client.

In your assessment it is important to identify psycho-social dysfunctions, not simply the pattern of ingestion of psychoactive substances. The two often correlate closely, but not always. There are people who consume vast amounts of psychoactive substances with few problems or dysfunctions. Conversely, there are those who use minute amounts of psychoactive substances, but lose control completely when they do so.

Be careful about biasing your assessment with the assumption that crack addicts are sociopaths who feel no guilt over their past drug use or street behaviors. There is a tendency for a counselor to react negatively to the extremely deviant behaviors recounted during the assessment. For example, a mother reported that her son was addicted to crack. He had been smoking it for a while, but it was getting out of control. I asked her how she came to that conclusion. "Well," she said, "this morning I woke up and saw our family car up on cinder blocks with all four tires missing. My son said he sold them for some rocks!" Men and women who walk into treatment programs have sold their bodies for rocks. One young girl told me that she had oral sex with a dope man for a fifty-cent hit on the pipe. In Florida, hundreds of "snow babies" are born each year; in the United States, thousands, conservatively. We wonder how a mother could use crack when she knows it will hurt, deform, or kill the child she is carrying. Even professionally trained counselors can react moralistically to these behaviors.

Although crack addicts behave in some bizarre, anti-social ways, we should not generalize and conclude that all crack addicts are sociopaths. Counselors know from their counseling sessions that most recovering crack addicts do feel remorse for their past behaviors, once they are de-toxed enough to realize what they did to survive on the streets. Crack addicts are incredibly adaptable persons, more so than sociopaths. They have lived in an ugly, dangerous, violent environment and survived. People do what they do to survive. From a drug-free, rational frame of reference, the behaviors of the crack addict seem, minimally, sociopathic. Try to see life through the eyes of clients. And never forget, "There, save by the grace of God, go I."

The assessment session should provide the counselor with facts about these important aspects of the addiction: presenting problem; history of the problem; family impact; functional strengths and deficits; medical history; and mental state.

Presenting problem. Addicts don't just wake up one morning and say, "Gosh, I think I'll quit smoking crack today, go into withdrawal and feel miserable." There is always a triggering event or an overpowering combination of events, a personal history, that has motivated the addict to seek counseling now. The counselor must discover the details of this event as part of the assessment process by asking questions like: What incident or event brought you in for professional help at this time? If a spouse or significant other has been the force causing the addict to seek help, make that person an ally. Such an ally can be important in keeping the addict motivated through treat-ment and recovery.

History of the problem. Ask specific questions when compiling a drug history. When did it all start? What is the present pattern of use? What is the frequency, duration and intensity of the use? Does the client define the problem as abuse, or addiction, and why? Ask if prescription and nonprescription medications also are used. Which one and how frequently? What about over-the-counter medications? Ask about the client's use of other drugs such as marijuana, beer, wine and wine coolers. Many crack addicts don't realize that these are drugs, too. If a client says he consumes "one or two drinks each night," ask about the size of a drink. Is it a four-ounce drink or a sixty-four ounce drink? Ask how he mixes the drinks. Are they mixed with fifty percent alcohol and fifty percent mixer, or a ninety-five-to-five mix?

The counselor must know the street terminology related to dosage. If a crack addict claims he is using an "eight ball" four times per week, do you know how much that is? Street drug terminology varies from one region of the country to another. For example, in some parts of Florida a "cookie" is one-sixteenth of an ounce of crack. In other parts of Florida, a "cookie" refers to a method of packaging crack, having nothing to do with weight. In parts of the United States a "love boat" or "juice joint" is marijuana mixed with crack cocaine. In other areas, such as the Caribbean Basin, this is called either "bait" or "black joints." Terminology changes so rapidly it would be useless to list it here. A counselor must rely on clients and co-workers to keep up with street drug terminology.

Family impact. Obtain information on the client's family-of-origin. What norms, rules and mores existed in that family regarding drug use, medications and drinking? In evaluating the client's current family, find the role drugging and drinking plays. How is crack affecting the family? Who is being affected? How has the family changed in trying to adjust to the problem? How does this injure specific family members? What can be expected to happen within the family system once the identified patient stops using drugs and alcohol? Predict how much support and sabotage may come from significant others during the client's treatment and recovery.

History of sobriety. What is your longest period of sobriety? Tell me about that time. The answer often will be: "I never had any sobriety or abstinence since I started using drugs." Challenge this. All addicts, even crack addicts, have had some success in abstaining, even if it was for a brief moment. Build on this success, even if it is modest. For example, once a client said, "Well, five years ago I went without drugs for six days."

"Great, you did something right. What were the circumstances and what did you do to not use?"

"I was in the hospital for six days."

"Okay, you could stop while you were in the hospital. Why was that?"

"I wasn't around anyone who was using and I didn't have access to drugs. If I'd had them around, I would have used them."

"Hey, don't minimize what you did. You learned that if you avoid drug users, and avoid being around the drug itself, you can remain drug free. That's great. Let's build our plan on this. We'll teach you how to avoid drug-using folks and how to recognize situations where drugs will be available."

Crack addicts routinely say they have attempted to stay off crack by locking themselves up in the house and avoiding their drug-using friends. They say this to convince the counselor of the futility of trying to stay "clean and sober." They claim that after two or three days of sobriety, they start going stir-crazy. A craving for cocaine is magnified by a craving for social contact. Reframe what they perceive as a failure in terms that convey hope. Reassure the crack addict that staying clean can work. Instead of hiding in the house day and night to avoid drug-using friends, the addict can spend time with other people who also are trying to stop using. These people can be found in treatment programs or in community support groups such as Cocaine Anonymous.

Functional strengths and deficits. Focus on both positives and negatives. Does the client have developmental deficits that preclude a short-term program and require a long-term habilitation model? Does the client have legal problems that might require him to leave a residential treatment program? Can an unresolved legal problem be used to motivate the client to continue with the recommended treatment? How well can the client read and write? Will the client's literacy level reduce the likelihood of benefiting from a treatment program requiring the use of workbooks, logs and essays?

Medical history. Find out if the client is experiencing any physical symptoms that warrant immediate medical attention. For example, if a crack-addicted client admits having used one hundred milligrams of Valium tranquilizer per day continuously for five years but now having stopped using two days ago feels "kinda weird," you should refer him immediately to a physician. If a client claims to have been dosing XTC and is on MAO inhibitors, get medical intervention. If the client confesses to a history of multiple closed-head traumas, and reports "fugues" or what appear to be blackouts, this will warrant a physician's attention. Many medical aspects of addiction are outside the counselor's realm of expertise. When in doubt about the significance of a physical symptom, refer the client to a physician experienced in addictions.

Mental state. We are all aware crack cocaine can cause behaviors that mimic true psychopathology. A detailed evaluation of a client's mental status usually is required upon admission to a treatment program, and again after detoxification. This involves assessing such things as level of functioning, suicidal risk or ideations, homicidal risk or ideations and any dysfunction in thoughts, moods or orientation. A thorough evaluation of the client's mental state is done by professionals with specialized training. Often this is beyond the scope and training of substance abuse counselors, hence, the need for referrals to ancillary staff. The mental status portion of an evaluation is the evaluator's opportunity to combine objective data and subjective impressions on the client's overall level of functioning. It may include assessment of intelligence, personality, and neurological functioning.

The way you approach the initial assessment with clients affects how they will respond to therapy in the future. Remember, counselors have been shown to be unable to predict, from initial assessments, who will be successful in treatment. But they sometimes *can* predict who will fail in treatment. This failure is often the result of the self-fulfilling prophecy effect. If a counselor believes an addict will fail in treatment, that belief may be conveyed to other professionals who will consciously or unconsciously alter their behavior toward the one in treatment. The judgment that a client can't succeed in treatment is an enormous obstacle to overcome. Assume everyone will make it. Learn to live with the sadness if they don't.

PLANNING

An Event and a Process

$\mathbf{P}$lanning is both an event and a process that unfolds from the initial assessment. The facts gathered during the assessment session should be used to help the client make an informed decision about treatment. No one enters a hospital with a headache and requests neurosurgery for the pain. The patient expects a physician to make an assessment and to explain alternative treatments such as medications, biofeedback, bibliotherapy on the topic of stress management, or in extreme cases, surgery. Counselors should do the same. We need to recommend a viable method, or methods, of treatment, including risks and costs.

After considering the facts gathered during the initial assessment, the counselor should quickly offer treatment recommendations to the crack addict and his family. In offering treatment recommendations, the counselor should carefully control the presentation. Counselors sometimes interpret the facts correctly and offer sound treatment recommendations, only to be frustrated by a client's unwillingness to accept them. This is less likely to happen if the counselor adopts a person-centered approach.

Explain Your Recommendations

An important rule for the counselor to follow in recommending a treatment program for a crack addict is to emphasize the criteria upon which your judgment is based. Avoid making bare pronouncements like, "Based on what you've told me, I *feel* a 28-day inpatient program is what you need." The client wants to hear your reactions to and interpretations of his problem in the language and context of your experience and knowledge as an expert in the field of addictions treatment. Synthesize the data and see how it fits into the goals established by yourself and the client.

For example, assume a client comes into your office and your initial assessment discloses these facts:

Presenting problem: "I want to stop all drugs so my spouse won't leave me."

Drug(s) of abuse: crack and alcohol.

Frequency of use: five days per week.

Intensity of crack use: two-to-three grams per episode.

Intensity of alcohol use: six beers while using crack, each episode.

Duration of alcohol and crack use: six months.

Longest period of abstinence: three days.

Family dysfunction: spouse filed for divorce but will stop the process if client gets help.

Medical history: nothing relevant.

Mental status: client acts out with violence toward spouse when intoxicated. No history of violence when not intoxicated.

Vocational history: worked in federal GS position for past twelve years. Still employed.

Education: two years of college.

Legal Complications: none.

The following is an illustration of how a counselor could frame treatment recommendations to gain the addict's involvement and minimize resistance.

Based on the information you gave me, I recommend that you consider two treatment alternatives. I do believe you need professional assistance in stopping cocaine use. I recommend you consider either inpatient detoxification followed by structured evening treatment, or inpatient residential services for four to six weeks. Let me explain why.

First, you're using crack, a highly addictive substance. It's very difficult to stop without being in a structured environment. Crack is too readily available on the streets. The "cues" or triggers you developed over the past six months could lead you to use it again.

For you, total abstinence should be the goal. You are too deeply involved with crack and alcohol to be a social user again. I also don't believe that your relationship with your spouse could tolerate many more episodes of drug use. You both told me you want to stay together, so I'll make a recommendation on the safe side. I suggest inpatient detoxification. Your body will be going through

117

many changes when you stop the cocaine and alcohol. You need to have a good medical work-up and observation during this period. You will experience cravings for cocaine after a few days. This is normal, and a good sign because it means your body is getting back to a normal state and trying to get used to that.

Second, I recommend inpatient detoxification to give you some cool-down time. You're enmeshed in conflict now. You have resentments, disappointments, anger, sadness, and frustration. Both of you feel these things now. Most people need some time to disengage from each other and to get their lives in order.

I also recommend structured outpatient services after the detoxification. This is a program that meets five times per week for three hours each session, for four weeks. It's a family program, which means both you and your spouse should participate if it is to work well. During this program, you'll both be involved in family education, counseling sessions and group sessions. You'll both learn skills to improve your lives. You'll also both be introduced to community support groups.

The other alternative is inpatient residential treatment. This program lasts four to six weeks. It includes detoxification and treatment in a structured environment. The main difference is that this option will keep you in a structured program, away from temptations and triggers, while you receive counseling and learn new skills to help you remain drug free.

There is a trade-off. With the first option, you will be an outpatient client and have access to drugs and alcohol. This could lead to a slip.

It's time now to discuss these things. Decide if your relationship could survive another slip. Consider if you both are willing to make a commitment to treatment together. I want to put you in the treatment environment that interferes least with your lives. That would be structured evening treatment, but only if both of you can make a commitment to the program for the full four weeks. If you doubt that, go inpatient for four to six weeks.

We don't need a definite decision now. What we can do, and I recommend it, is to get you inpatient for the medical services and detoxification for about a week. After that week, we can discuss further whether your plan will include inpatient residential or evening treatment.

Five important treatment principles are illustrated here.

1. The counselor explained the reasons for the recommendations.
2. Treatment options were presented with the pluses and minuses for each.
3. Alternatives were reasonable and would have a good chance of leading to successful recovery.
4. The client was given a sense of personal power by being directly involved in the decision process.
5. The client didn't assume the counselor's role by writing the treatment plan.

Planning is also an important part of outpatient counseling. These treatment plans vary in format, but generally include three components: the stated problem(s), the goals of treatment for each problem area defined, and the methods of remediating the identified problems and attaining the identified goals.

Problems	Goals/objectives	Methods
What are the issues to work on?	What do you want to happen?	How are you going to do it?

Treatment plans should be SMART: Specific, Measurable, Attainable, Relevant, and Time-framed. Otherwise, they are dream sheets, not treatment plans. Plans which are not SMART often are weak, worthless or even damaging because they articulate goals that are impossible to reach, exposing the addict to the risk of yet another failure. Before I show you a SMART treatment plan, let's consider one that isn't.

A Weak Plan

The following is an example of a weak treatment plan with many flaws:

Problems	Goals/objectives	Methods
drugs	drug free for life	outpatient counseling
family	good relationship with family	family counseling

poor self-con- cept	positive self- concept	counseling

The problem is described as "drugs," without specifying the degree of the problem: use, abuse, or dependency. It does not identify the type(s) of drug(s) ingested, nor the frequency, duration or intensity of use. The first goal is to remain "drug free for life." How do we measure progress toward that goal? Achievement of this goal can only be fully confirmed upon death. The treatment method, "outpatient counseling," doesn't specify how often, what kind, the length of each session or the projected duration of the intervention.

The second problem noted in the plan, "family," has the same weaknesses as the first one. It is not specific enough. The goal of a "good relationship with family" is unmeasurable, rarely attainable as stated, and not placed within a realistic time frame.

The third problem is "poor self-concept." Self-concept is a phenomenological construct, intangible and unmeasurable. The goal of achieving a "positive self-concept" is vague. Does this mean the person can only be considered to have successfully completed this goal if he always feels good about himself?

A SMART Plan

Here is a treatment plan that meets the SMART criteria. Compare the plan's elements with the earlier plan and you will note that the problems and goals are spelled out clearly and that the methods to be used are precise and measurable:

Problems	Goals/objectives	Methods
cocaine dependency 2-3 grams, smoked 3 times per week for past 18 months continuously	remain drug free (no psychoactive medications or alcohol) while in the inpatient program	1. detox as per medical order 2. urinalysis 2-3x/wk random

After your treatment plan is developed reevaluate it periodically. Having a current plan maintains the focus during individual sessions and prevents the session from becoming sidetracked by smoke screen crises. The process of continually updating your treatment plan also validates client accomplishments. It shows evidence of progress, confirming the success of the counselor's work and suggesting a change of direction if one is needed.

Unfortunately, clients do not always comply with a counselor's recommendations. When this occurs, counselors can be more successful by seducing clients into getting better than by forcing them to get better. Sometimes clients refuse treatment. If a crack addict refuses treatment, use a feedback model. Note the client's dysfunctional behaviors and his own goals and aspirations. Then ask the client to explain the discrepancy between the two. Ask him about his plan for solving his problems and why it hasn't worked. Try to sell the client your path to his dreams.

Finally, if a client flatly refuses to follow your recommendations, ask him to agree to a behavioral contract (see Chapter 10). Establish goals and ask him to agree that if he fails to achieve those goals, using his method, he will then follow your treatment recommendations. This way the counselor sets up contingencies so that if the client's plan proves successful, he wins. If unsuccessful, there remains a built-in backup plan for success: your original treatment recommendation. This provides freedom, but within limits.

10

GROUP THERAPY

Living With Others

Group therapy is probably the most widely used treatment for chemical dependency. For crack addicts, however, group therapy presents several special problems stemming from their not having shared feelings, thoughts, and behaviors openly for a long time. Group therapy is a foreign experience, something completely antithetical to the norms they conformed to as addicts. Had they behaved on the streets like they are expected to in group therapy, they would not have survived. Instead of the sharing and openness that is the goal of group therapy, crack addicts have learned to pull into themselves, censoring and blocking genuine human interactions. Group therapy teaches crack addicts how to live *with* others again.

Preparing the Addict for Group Work

An important reason that crack addicts don't do therapy right is that they haven't had any practice. To increase the effectiveness of group therapy, carefully prepare the crack addict for this experience. Don't just place him in group therapy and hope for the best. Begin to lay the ground-work for group therapy while your client is still in the assessment and treatment planning stages of therapy. Use pamphlets, video tapes, audio tapes and face-to-face discussion.[1]

Group therapy looks easy and certain individuals are thought to have a special gift for guiding sessions. Neither is true. Counselors with no formal or professional training in group therapy, but who are attempting to direct sessions, should seek formal training at a training institution. A homemade, do-it-yourself approach to group therapy can actually undermine sobriety and adjustment. Formal training in group work shows how being a great group therapy leader is a learned skill, not an inherent, intuitive virtue.[2]

At the start of group therapy, establish guidelines or rules. One strategy is to create a contract, a list of standards of conduct for all persons in the group. Basic elements of a contract are: confidentiality; the right to pass on any group exercise; rules about feedback; rules about starting and stopping on time; and rules about violence or threats of violence. Going much beyond these basic agreements puts a straight jacket on the group, with everyone

---

1. See, for example, I. R. Elder, *Group Psychotherapy: A Client Orientation - A Video* (Bradenton, FL: Human Services Institute, 1990).

2. See the classic book on group therapy: Irving Yalom. *The Theory and Practice of Group Psychotherapy*, (New York: Basic Books, 1985).

being afraid to act spontaneously because it might violate the contract. The counselor should develop the contract. Allow members to add one or two additional rules (if they are realistic), but do not allow the group to make the rules. Crack cocaine addicts have a tendency to overcontrol. When they finish their own list there would be one thousand rules. Group members would become so legalistic that no real work could take place.

After completing the rules for group therapy sessions, with or without group input, ask each member to sign the list. Post it on the wall of the meeting room. It is a constant reminder that everyone has seen the rules and agreed to comply. Later, in weeks to follow, use this contract as an intervention. If someone starts to violate the contract, simply say, "Please look at Number Six. You agreed to comply with that rule." Use a brief, nonabrasive intervention.

Growth Stages

Stage One. Once the group contract is established, start working the group through the stages of growth. In Stage One, group members will show much dependence on you as the group leader. The counselor should accept that leadership role and be somewhat autocratic. Set norms for the group and reinforce members who comply. Do not act nondirective or laissez-faire with a beginning group of crack addicts. In fact, the group usually won't let the leader operate as a passive, laissez-faire leader. The following illustrates what I mean.

A counselor walks into a beginning group and says, "This is your group. What do you want to do?" This is a big mistake. One of two things will happen. The group will sit motionless and do nothing until the frustrated counselor takes control, or the group will begin to slide into chaos until the counselor becomes frustrated and takes control. Either way the counselor eventually takes control. Beginning groups need a firm leader to show each member that it is a controlled, safe environment led by a competent professional.

Stage Two. Once the counselor is established as the leader and the group trusts that leadership, group members will start to test each other to see if everyone is strong enough to handle their problems. They are now a Stage Two group, testing the water. They typically do this through intragroup conflict. They engage in conflict to see how much heart each member has, how much commitment.

This is the proverbial test of fire for group members. The leader was tested in Stage One. Now it's the group's turn. The leader lets the conflicts evolve, not interfering unless there is a danger of physical violence. The leadership should change from autocratic, in Stage One, to more democratic in Stage Two where interactions should be primarily between and among members. Allow group members to communicate directly with each other, not through the counselor as in Stage One. If the group tries to establish the norm that interactions must go through the group leader, block it. It may help to avoid eye contact with members who want all interactions to go through the leader. Use some joining techniques. Make statements like, "Susan, when you said that to Jim, I noticed Sally and Tom nodded in agreement." This joins people together by connecting their names.

The group leader has considerable influence and power. Use this power to establish norms by reinforcing appropriate behaviors. When a group member does what is desired, reinforce him. Other clients are then more likely to do the right thing to obtain approval. If your group begins to disintegrate through continuing conflict, it is a sign that the leader set norms inappropriately in Stage One. Stage Two is a trust-developing stage, so let them do it. Also remember that if a group seems cohesive, but never experiences any intragroup conflict, they probably are just a polite Stage One group.

Stage Three. Stage Three is the cohesive stage, characterized by work getting done, free exchange and interactions between members, and laissez-faire or democratic leadership by the group leader. This is the time for the counselor to keep quiet. Let the clients do the work. The counselor's work was setting the rules and norms in the first two stages. Now the group is in control of itself. Of course, if a crisis comes up that is beyond the scope of the group, the professional has the responsibility to intervene and take charge. The counselor is responsible for each member of the group, for each one's emotional and physical safety.

Stage Four. Stage Four is the winding down stage. Members are about to leave the group and unsupported go back out into the real world. The issues in Stage Four surround disengagement from the group, self-doubt over being able to survive in the real world without therapy group members, and issues involving loss and separation. It may help at this time to reassert strong leadership to normalize the fears and apprehensions of the members.

Rarely do groups begin at Stage One and progress intact through Stage Four. Most chemical dependency counselors work with open-ended groups whose members arrive and leave weekly, sometimes more frequently. Despite being in a constant state of flux, open-ended groups still grow in stages. They move up and down from Stage One to Stage Two to Stage Three and back to Stage One. Each time a new member joins the group, members revert to Stage One to begin the group process of testing and dependency. With one new client per week entering the group, the effect may be short-lived. The group will regress back to Stage One, pick up a new member emotionally, test him, have conflict with him, and return to Stage Three in a short time. The more extensive and rapid the changes in group membership, the more likely it is that the group will regress to earlier stages of growth and stay there longer.

Counselors, often equate a good group with one that is cohesive, humming with frequent and free interactions between members, in other words, a Stage Three group. It is easy to feel frustrated when working in environments (many residential treatment programs) that have open-ended groups. They always seem stuck in Stage Two with some flirting toward cohesion in Stage Three. Often counselors think they are nonproductive. This isn't true.

Stage Two is the stage that concerns testing limits with peers and learning how to handle conflict through methods other than avoidance or aggression. It is the stage that teaches trust in others. What better lessons for clients to learn in a group situation? Stage Three is clean and cohesive. There is much sharing and caring. There are great self-disclosures with supportive feedback offered and received. However, learning to trust another human and to respect differences, without running away or becoming too aggressive, are essential lessons for crack addicts.

Group Composition

There is debate over homogeneous versus heterogeneous group composition, whether a group's members should have similar backgrounds, problems and issues, or whether a diversity in backgrounds is better. The best answer is, "It depends on the group's mission." When a group is intended to be more an educational experience than a therapy experience, it helps to have a high degree of homogeneity. A group concerning "coping with HIV," would be more effective as a homogeneous group of persons affected by the virus. A group on "crack use among pregnant women," may need to be composed only of women. A group on the importance of male role models in recovery for the recovering adolescent male may target a homogeneous group composed only of adolescent males.

Heterogeneous groups usually are preferable for therapy. The diversity stimulates thinking and minimizes a coat-tailing effect that can occur among people of similar backgrounds. An example of coat-tailing occurred in a program with a methadone component. The outpatient staff had begun a methadone client group. It was not working well and group leaders were frustrated with clients. A counselor described the problem as, "All those clients want to talk about is their dosage of methadone. They won't stay on the topic of addiction and recovery."

This is understandable when you consider that methadone was the common denominator used in selecting group members. That is the one element they could join together on in the early stages of group therapy. A group of drug-addicted, short people in a group therapy session would talk more about height than about drug addiction. A group of alcoholic Marines would talk about the Marines as much as about their addiction.

If a counselor wanted the methadone group to explore issues surrounding addiction and recovery it would have been better to create a heterogeneous group including methadone maintenance clients, methadone detoxification clients, recovering methadone detoxification clients who have some total abstinence under their belt, recovering alcoholics and recovering cocaine addicts. The focus would shift from, "We're all drinking methadone so let's talk about that," to "We're all addicts so let's talk about that." You still provide a common denominator, but it is more focused toward a recovery goal than a method (milligrams of methadone).

Self-Oriented Behaviors

Self-oriented behaviors (SOBs) frustrate counselors guiding group therapy. SOBs are client behaviors focused on controlling the therapy group's process and content. Clients use self-oriented behaviors to protect themselves from other group members. They want to establish group norms that are consistent with their level of comfort. They are not bad, just scared. There is often a tendency for the addict who experiences these feelings to avoid participating in the group or to become a disruptive force.

A typical SOB involves the presentation of self. When anyone goes into a group therapy session, or any new social group for that matter, they enter with a certain image they wish to present. Everyone has an ideal self that they hope people in the new group will see. That ideal self may be "the smartest person" or "the junior counselor" or "the sexiest person" or even "the biggest bad-ass of the group."

Unfortunately, an individual cannot always impound his chosen ideal self to keep someone else from taking it. For instance, suppose you wanted to be seen as the smartest person in a group, but during the introduction of members you heard another person tell the group, "I am Dr. Doe. I am a physician and attorney with a Ph.D. in physics." Your chance to present your ideal self, "the smartest" role, vanishes. You would feel insecure, scared, threatened, structureless, rudderless. There is a tendency for the addict who experiences these feelings to avoid participating in the group or to become a disruptive force. This kind of behavior is a clue that structure and direction are needed. A SOB needs to know that he's safe, and that the leader accepts him for who he is, even if the SOB doesn't know himself.

A sensitive counselor can turn the negativity of the SOB into a positive group experience. For example, there were two men in a therapy training group. Both were great people, but both had very similar ideal selves that they wanted to present. Both wanted to be the "bad boy" of the group. The first locked this role up and, of course, the second went into an identity crisis. He was quiet and withdrawn for an hour or so.

About then, the group began addressing the issue of role identity. The estranged bad boy smiled. When openly talked about by the group, he admitted feeling lost when he couldn't lock up his role. In doing this he assumed a new and unique role: the first person to self-disclose. Instead of being the bad boy of the group, he was the risk taker. We all were happy after that and the group began to hum.

INDIVIDUAL COUNSELING

Key Features for Crack Addicts

Individual counseling is a successful and widely used treatment method in the chemical dependency field. Both group therapy and individual counseling are beneficial in the treatment of crack addiction, but in different ways. What can be achieved in individual sessions often cannot be done in a group format, and vice versa.

Individual counseling is the ideal modality for performing specialized types of therapy like covert conditioning. Covert conditioning involves modifying behavior through operant conditioning administered during hypnotic or deep relaxation states. This requires individually-tailored methods, so it cannot be done as effectively in a group setting. Another specialized method of treatment, which works best in individual sessions, is systematic desensitization. Other types of therapy, such as journaling or charting behavior, are also optimized in individual sessions.

The key features of individual counseling for crack addicts are: (1) joining with the client and establishing trust; (2) collecting client data from which to develop a treatment plan; (3) resolving or "de-crising" issues that are too emotionally charged to discuss in groups; (4) motivating the client toward participation in group-centered treatment; (5) contracting with new clients as a method of early intervention; and, (6) teaching skills or conducting therapy that is incongruent with a group format.

Establishing Trust

Join with the client and establish trust. It is imperative to do this quickly. It is tempting to deal with issues during the first few minutes of the first counseling session, but there will be time for this once the stage is set by establishing a trusting relationship. Crack addiction is a disease of chemically induced selfishness. Those who develop a compulsion to use this chemical substance sacrifice human relationships for the addictive relationship. Addiction is a disease of isolation. The first requirement for recovery is to establish a trusting human relationship with another breathing, feeling, caring person. The counselor can be important in fulfilling this need. Therefore, I spend most of the first session, and a part of each subsequent session, joining with the client socially.

Collecting Client Data

Individual counseling sessions provide an ideal environment in which to collect information vital to the therapy process. Sensitivity is the basic requirement for the counselor seeking information from crack addicted clients. It is essential that counselors respect the crack addict's boundaries and values.

Counselors repeatedly do assessments and engage in individual counseling sessions. In the process, professionals sometimes become desensitized to how their words or questions may be emotionally charged. For example, a counselor may ask a client: "How do you afford drugs? Are you stealing, dealing, using your kids' food money, or, maybe, turning tricks?" Well, the addict may be doing these things to support the habit, but to admit it to a stranger is difficult, and embarrassing. Counselors must remember that, although we may be desensitized to these revelations after working with thousands of addicts, clients are not desensitized to the embarrassment of self-disclosing that information to us.

Resolving Issues

Individual counseling offers a unique opportunity to resolve, or at least de-crisis problems and events in a crack addict's life, events that immobilize him and prevent him from adapting to group therapy. Traumatic issues that are common among crack addicts include childhood sexual, emotional and physical abuse. Other issues that may need to be de-crisised during individual sessions to improve clients' ability to function include: anger versus violence, sexual identity, physical challenges or conditions (e.g. HIV), racism, and past negative experiences in group therapy.

Although it is critical to prepare people for group therapy by de-crisising certain issues, this too must be done carefully. Many traumatic issues will not be resolvable in a few sessions. A good example of this is incest, a psychologically damaging experience typically requiring long-term work. For someone with a trauma that can't be quickly resolved, evaluate whether group counseling would be beneficial and if it would be desirable to have concurrent individual sessions on the crisis issue. Also, consider referring this addict to a specialist in the particular crisis area.

Crack addicts often generate new crisis issues to stay within the known and controllable environment of individual counseling. Avoid becoming so wrapped up in crisis issues that the addict becomes locked into individual counseling sessions as the only form of chemical dependency treatment.

Motivating Clients for Group Therapy

Individual counseling should inform crack-addicted clients of the purpose and benefits of group counseling, teaching them the skills required for successful participation. Many programs do an admirable job of preparing crack addicts for the group therapy experience. These programs use videotapes of group sessions, observed and processed by the counselor and client within the security of individual sessions. Some provide printed materials explaining the stages of group growth, what to expect during each stage, the role of the group leader, roles often adopted by the members, and common problems such as role identification and self-disclosure. Some programs encourage clients to practice group skills, such as confrontation, during individual sessions. Some give clients a list of the basic ground rules for group participation and go over a sample group contract during individual counseling sessions.

It is also important to spend some time with crack addicts exploring the fears and apprehensions that may be a source of resistance to group therapy. Common fears are: being attacked, self-disclosing too much, being rejected, having a problem nobody else has, becoming angry, violent, crying, or losing control. Often, by simply reviewing this list with crack addicts during an individual session, counselors can normalize the apprehension and increase motivation for group treatment.

Raising the Bottom

Every counselor has clients in individual counseling who need other services or other treatment modalities, but refuse them. Individual counseling is an ideal environment for providing early intervention for those clients who see no need for additional treatment. Behavioral contracts can help raise the bottom for these clients.

For example, John Doe is an individual counseling client who desperately needs to be in group therapy, possibly even inpatient treatment. He is a crack user, using two to three grams per episode, twice a week for two years before coming into treatment. John tested positive for crack four times during the past six months in counseling. Each time he did great work in the individual session, explored his feelings about using and made emotional amends through many cathartic sessions. But he still is an accident waiting to happen. He has great intentions but is addicted. A possible solution is to write the following behavioral contract with John.

> I, John Doe, agree to attend individual therapy sessions three times per week for the next six weeks. During this time I will not use any psycho-active substances. During this time I will leave random urine samples for testing. I have also signed a release to my probation officer. After this six-week period, I will cut back my sessions to twice a week for the next six weeks. Should I not remain drug free, as measured by a positive urinalysis, or if I miss any session, I agree to the following:
>
> 1. To attend Cocaine Anonymous groups twice a week for six consecutive weeks.
> 2. To attend group counseling twice a week for six consecutive weeks.
> 3. To attend individual counseling once each week for six consecutive weeks.
>
> Signed by _____
> Witnessed by counselor: _____
> Date_____

The behavioral contract is nothing more than a short-term treatment plan aimed at a specific behavior. Therefore, it should comply with the SMART rules for the development of a treatment plan described in Chapter 9.

Avoiding Isolation

Individual counselors in a chemical dependency treatment facility often work apart from the rest of the agency. They see clients eight hours a day in a small, isolated cubicle, or office. There are times when they are unsure about how to proceed with a particular case and need input from other professionals. There are other times when they are so successful that they need to share their pride in their work. A feeling of isolation is a common frustration of counselors who work primarily alone.

To counteract this feeling of isolation, counselors need the opportunity to do co-therapy with another counselor. This could be co-led family therapy, co-led group counseling or even co-led individual therapy. This counseling partnership can benefit both the client and the counselor. Another option to reduce the sense of isolation is to bring a colleague into an individual session as a consultant. This outside expert can validate the counselor's work, point out deficits that may exist in the clinical relationship, and have a strong impact on the client.

Finally, no one can do it all. No one's skills, no matter how polished, are extensive enough to handle all issues or problems that might arise in chemical dependency counseling. Referring a crack addicted client to another professional with special skills is a sign of your competence and good judgment.

PSYCHOEDUCATION

Building Skills for Recovery

Many lectures, films, and seminars used in the chemical dependency field do nothing more than pass a few hours. There is little value in showing, to a crack addict, a film on the dangers of drugs, on the classification of drugs, on the physiological effects of alcohol on the human system, or on the etiology of addiction. That has real value in education and prevention but not much in primary treatment. Simple films that say "don't do this," are not going to work with someone who has every aspect of his life entangled with a psychoactive substance. The emphasis in treatment for crack addiction needs to be on teaching new skills, not trying to convince addicts that their old skills are destructive or bad.

Psychoeducation, a crucial skill-building element in treating addiction to crack, focuses on the three domains of learning: affective, cognitive and psychomotor. Clinical staff members who have worked as professional educators will often have had experience in developing and delivering pschoeducational materials under the rubric "affective education."

People retain best what they do, not what they hear, read or see. Good psychoeducation needs to be hands-on. Each psychoeducational seminar should have goals, objectives, methods, materials, instructions for delivery and handouts clearly delineated for the instructor.

Professional counselors are probably familiar with the basic psychoeducational topics that should be explored with crack addicts. Many of these topics also are relevant to other addictions. The most important topics for a psychoeducational program are:

Decision Making	Relapse Triggers (avoidance)
Assertion	Relapse Triggers (desensitize)
Conflict Management	Communication Skills
Moods/Anger	Learning to Ask for Help

It is not necessary for each program to develop its own psychoeducational seminars. Chemical dependency treatment has now reached the point where there are reams of psychoeducational literature and materials available to professionals. Many chemical dependency counselors will find it more cost-effective to purchase published workbooks and materials than to develop their own. Still, however, some counselors may want to develop materials especially for their own programs or to add to the chemical dependency literature. Developing psychoeducational seminars can be a fulfilling experience resulting in a product of lasting value. Staff persons often prefer delivering psychoeducational seminars for which they have a feeling of ownership.

12: PSYCHOEDUCATIONAL SKILLS

When developing psychoeducational seminars, be sure that the materials and methodology focus on all three domains of learning. Doing so will result in better retention of skills. The following example illustrates the development of a psychoeducational seminar. This will be an assertion seminar using the three domains, affective, cognitive, and psychomotor, to teach the crack addict to "Just Say No."

The seminar could begin with a lecture (cognitive) on the difference between being assertive and being aggressive. Two people in the group might then do a role play in which one stands on a table and says "Do it, do it!" while the other kneels below and says passively, "Okay, anything you say, anything you say." Before long the person kneeling on the floor begins to experience powerful feelings (affective). Then, both role-players share their feelings with the group. Next, the group breaks into pairs. While standing one foot apart, looking into each other's eyes, the members of each pair take turns saying loudly, "No!" (psychomotor). Finally, the entire group reassembles and talks about the feelings each had when saying and hearing "No!" (affective).

In this example, a counselor would have spent one hour with the group teaching assertiveness through the cognitive, affective and psychomotor domains. In follow-up seminars, the counselor could teach thought-stopping techniques (psychomotor) and S.U.D. levels (subjective units of discomfort) for clients to use when in situations requiring assertiveness (cognitive). The crack addicts may role-play events when they sold out (affective). Then the

counselor could ask addicts to replay the scenario asser-
tively (psychomotor). The possibilities are numerous.

Deaddiction

A buzz word in the crack cocaine treatment field is
"deaddiction." This term typically encompasses covert
conditioning and desensitization, and some behavioral
thought-stopping and mood-management techniques. Deaddiction has real potential in skill-building for relapse
prevention. An example of a deaddiction program follows.

During the first session, the dynamics of craving are
discussed. Crack addicts learn that most relapses are not
due to drug craving. Addicts learn that environmental
triggers, more than any other event, cause relapse. These
environmental triggers may be sights, sounds, smells, or
tastes that were associated with past crack cocaine use
and, when they occur, they immediately restimulate
thoughts of crack use. Crack-addicted clients are told that
they can do two things to minimize the effects of these
environmental triggers. They can avoid all potential
triggers, a difficult, if not impossible, task. Some of these
triggers are so subtle, unconscious, that voluntary avoidance of them is unrealistic. Or second, they can learn to
control their reaction to these triggers, reducing the power
of subtle environmental cues. The main insight of the first
session is that learning to control reactions to triggers is
the most effective way of managing recovery. This topic
involves primarily the cognitive domain.

Session Number Two is devoted to teaching mood management techniques with a concentration on the affective and psychomotor domains. We might begin the session with some sensitivity exercises to teach crack addicts to identify bodily feelings, leading to an ability to recognize feelings of anxiety. We teach this psychoeducational skill by having the client progressively relax and then think of a past anxiety-provoking situation. Then we discuss the feelings experienced when they thought of the disturbing event. By the end of Session Two, crack addicts can identify feelings of anxiety and relaxation. As homework, between Sessions Two and Three, crack addicts practice the relaxation techniques that they have learned in Session Two. They practice relaxation each evening before they fall asleep.

Session Three is a repetition of Session Two, with some differences. Again, we practice relaxation while recalling anxiety-provoking events, but this time, we try to recall different anxiety provokers. After the exercise, we teach the crack addicts about SUDs, *subjective units of discomfort*. These are subjective measures of anxiety, on a one-to-one hundred-point scale. From this exercise the client may learn that memories of striking a lighter to a crack pipe caused a SUD of fifty, whereas memories of driving past the crack house caused a SUD of seventy-five. Crack addicts are now learning to discriminate between levels of anxiety.

Session Four focuses on further developing the addicts' progressive relaxation techniques, and teaching the behavioral technique of thought stopping. The addicts are instructed to progressively relax and then to recall an anxiety-provoking event. They are instructed to stay with the anxiety provoking thought until they feel a S.U.D.s level that is approaching unmanageability. Then they are instructed to visualize a stop sign in their mind, to yell mentally the word "stop," and to then return to the relaxation mode. This is repeated several times.

Session Five is a repeat of Session Four. Progressive relaxation is followed by recall of an anxiety provoker, then the use of thought stopping and, finally, a return to relaxation. If the group is showing good progress, each addict may be asked to recall and practice thought stopping with new anxiety provokers. This will help them desensitize from more environmental cues or triggers.

Session Six is the first attempt at what is called *in vivo* conditioning. A common way of doing this is to expose the crack addicts to real triggers, not just mentally visualized triggers. Some programs pass around crack pipes and each addict holds the pipe, experiences the anxiety, thought-stops, relaxes, and passes the pipe to the next person. Some programs pass around a bag of white powder, or a butane lighter, and has the crack addicts desensitize to these specific triggers. Some programs drive addicts-in-treatment through crack town, and have them practice their techniques of mood management.

The premise underlying the techniques of deaddiction is this: It is impossible for the addict to avoid all environmental triggers that may cause relapse. Therefore, it is necessary to neutralize the power out of triggers that can be identified by teaching mood management (identifying SUD levels, thought stopping, and progressive relaxation). These skills can be used any time the addict confronts a trigger that has not previously been identified.

Covert conditioning is another method of accomplishing deaddiction—disengaging the conditioned stimulus or triggers from the response of drug-using.[1] Common triggers for crack addicts include seeing white powder, seeing any substance that looks like crack (pebbles, chips of soap, even pieces of macadamia nuts), driving through the same neighborhood where they used to cop drugs, or even the smell of a match or the sound of a butane lighter flicking. All these triggers, cues, or conditioned stimuli create an urge, a conditioned response, to go out and use again. Covert conditioning is a method of providing operant conditioning through visual imagery, relaxation, or hypnosis.

The wonderful aspect of covert conditioning is that the addict can experience interacting with a drug environment while sitting in the safety of the therapist's office. The

---

1. In the late 1960s, at Boston College, a great deal of research was conducted on treating drug addicts by covert conditioning. There is a resurgence of interest in the application of covert conditioning with addicts, since the crack epidemic and the acknowledgment of failures in treating this population. Some excellent sources on this topic are: J.R. Cautela, "Covert Processes and Behavior Modification," *Journal of Nervous and Mental Diseases* 157, no.1(1973): 27-36; D. Upper, ed., *Covert Conditioning* (New York: Pergamon Press, 1979).

addict can confront drugs, feel the urges, reject them, and be reinforced, all within a safe environment. The addict can practice new behaviors that will generalize to the real world in an office, just as if it they were practiced in the real world. Covert conditioning works best if done in individual sessions and not in psychoeducational groups. It has been experimentally tested in group sessions with some positive results, but its usefulness is limited.

PROGRAM EXCELLENCE

You Can Be Effective with Crack Addicts

Not all crack addicts need twenty-eight day inpatient services combined with group therapy. It is important that each program and each modality of treatment, residential, individual counseling, group therapy, family therapy and so forth, have clear cut admission and discharge criteria and that the counselor be aware of them. When admission criteria are clear and precise, it is possible to prescribe the most appropriate treatment for each crack addict.

It is up to each treatment program to develop realistic, measurable, behavioral criteria to control the admission and discharge of the client, by modalities. Note that the criteria should follow the SMART rule: (S)pecific, (M)easurable, (A)ttainable, (R)elevant, and (T)ime-framed. For example, appropriate criteria for admissions into structured evening treatment might be:

1. self-stated or documented history of drug use;
2. self-stated or documented unsuccessful treatment in a less-restrictive environment such as outpatient treatment;

3. medical condition that permits detoxification or stabilization without inpatient medical supervision;
4. educational and vocational development consistent with chronological age; and,
5. designated family or significant other support and willingness of this support to participate in the evening treatment process.

Criteria for discharge from this same evening treatment program might be:

1. attendance at evening treatment services as scheduled at the rate of 85 percent;
2. drug- and alcohol-free as determined by random urinalysis;
3. written and approved aftercare and continuing care plan; and,
4. verification of obtaining a CA (AA, NA) sponsor.

To go even beyond these criteria for admission and discharge, the program staff might want to use some scales developed for this specific purpose. Dr. David Mee-Lee, has developed some good criteria-based admission and discharge indicators for substance abusers, by modalities.[1]

Some professionals maintain that addiction is addiction: People addicted to alcohol, benzos, opiates, or crack

---

1. The instrument is called the RAATE Scale. D. Mee-Lee. "An Instrument for Treatment Progress and Matching: The Recovery Attitude and Treatment Evaluator (RAATE)," *Journal of Substance Abuse Treatment* 5, no.3 (1988): 183-186.

operate under the same basic dynamics. I find that crack addicts have characteristics that appear stronger and more consistently than they do among other addicts. These characteristics are not all negatives. To begin with, counselors have considerable leverage when working with crack addicts because they are more likely to admit a need for treatment than are other addicts. This may be because addiction to crack is so intense, so rapid in onset, and so immediately debilitating that they hit bottom and feel a need for help before having a chance to build elaborate defenses. There are, on the other hand, serious challenges for counselors.

Bringing the Street Into Treatment

Often, crack addicts bring the street with them into treatment. By this I mean that crack addicts are grandiose, pushy and noncompliant. They try to write their treatment plan and won't listen to anyone else's opinion. Counselors find it difficult to counsel a client who challenges everything they say. Crack addicts have a way of testing limits at every turn, and sometimes counselors feel more like jailers than therapists. Counselors who face this day after day sometimes would sooner see the client leave treatment "Against Medical Advice" (AMA) than to have to deal with this attitude for another three or four weeks.

Two Options. A counselor has two options when working with an addict who is grandiose, pushy and noncompliant: confrontation or creative affirmation. The counselor who chooses the first option confronts the client and attempts to overpower him. He puts crack addicts in their place, sets tight limits or breaks them down, and makes them realize they aren't as smart as they think they are. This counselor confronts the crack addicts' grandiosity in group therapy and reveals their true incompetence to peers. He pops the overinflated balloon, lets out all the crack addicts' hot air and leaves the torn remnants behind, to be molded into the right shape. This is unproductive. The addict is broken by the time he enters treatment. From day one in treatment everything a counselor does should be aimed at building up clients' self-concepts.

The counselor's second option is to find something positive to build on in these characteristics, affirming the strengths. What people interpret as pathology is often nothing more than unfocused virtue. How can we transform aggressive grandiosity into a positive attribute?

Consider a crack addict who challenges everything a group leader says and disrupts a group's dynamics by insisting that he knows more about addiction than anyone else because of his experiences on the street. He loudly interrupts others, minimizing their feelings and opinions by name-calling. The therapist uses all the normal intervention methods: The group is reminded of the contract that states "no interrupting others," and "respect others' opinions," but the behaviors continue. The counselor approaches the crack addict during a break. They discuss and reinforce group rules, but the problem behaviors continue. The counselor tries to avoid confronting this addict directly, hoping that other members will do it within the context of the group. But this is a stage one group. It doesn't happen.

The counselor knows that behavior is amazingly consistent and the chances are that this client exhibited these same behaviors on the street. He has probably been confronted before about being pushy, grandiose and non-compliant. So, instead of confronting him, the counselor reframes the crack addict's disruptive behavior. He responds by saying:

> *We are all here in this group to find out better ways to live our lives without getting strung out on crack, or going to jail. I'm glad to hear so many of you voice your thoughts and feelings about addiction and recovery.*
>
> *What is really great is the variety of ways you all express your opinions. Some of you are quiet. You may be especially sensitive to others' feelings and don't want to offend anyone. That's considerate, but I encourage you to speak up. Others of you are exactly the opposite. You may be loud at times, even interrupting others, and that tells me you must really feel like you need to be heard. You have some things to say that are very important to you. How can we, as a group, work things out so that the quiet folks feel more comfortable in speaking up, and the louder people feel heard without having to shout or interrupt others?*

By reframing the behaviors of all group members, the counselor joins the clients together. If he had confronted the addict directly, he would have polarized the group and produced even more defensiveness, pushiness and noncompliance.

Another way of dealing with the grandiose, noncompliant and pushy crack addict is to empower that person with practical and therapeutically sound options. For example, two years ago a client, Sam, was that addict. Everyone on our treatment team hated to work with him because of his aggressiveness. Sam came to see me about ten days before his expected date of discharge from inpatient treatment. He demanded to be discharged within two days, "successfully," so he could visit with his children on the upcoming holiday weekend. He presented his request as a demand. "If you don't discharge me successfully in the next two days, I'm splitting the program," he threatened.

The team's first inclination was to tell Sam to go ahead and leave. If he wanted to leave A.M.A. and self-destruct, that was his choice. That reaction would not have been a good therapeutic intervention for Sam. We might have felt better ourselves by putting him in his place, but that is not our job. Our job is to make people functional, and to do that by getting them drug free. So, the staff met and brainstormed some therapeutic options and came up with a win-win intervention.

I asked Sam to come into my office. "Sam, I'm really glad you want to visit your family over the holidays. It shows me you're really working toward making amends for past behaviors, and toward rebuilding a support system. Great. But I'm also afraid if you leave treatment now, you'll self-destruct. You still need to have support and direction from our staff. I don't want to see you leave AMA.

"Here are two options we are willing to live with. Think about each, and make a decision by noon today. The first option is to stay here for another two weeks, finish the inpatient program, and then go to aftercare as we arranged in your discharge plan. I know you don't want to do this, but think about it.

"The second option is that we will administratively discharge you from inpatient treatment this Friday. You can visit your family, but you will need to sign a release so we can contact them beforehand to verify the visit and speak with them again afterward. You'll also need to be on Antabuse. I know crack is your drug-of-abuse, but you always use it with alcohol, which usually is a gateway drug to your crack use. For our peace of mind, you need to be on Antabuse. When you come back, you will need to be in our structured outpatient program for four weeks. This meets four hours per night, four times per week. We also will do random urinalysis during this period.

"When you complete the four weeks of structured outpatient, we'll graduate you successfully from the inpatient and structured outpatient program, mainstreaming you into aftercare. Consider both options. Again, I don't want you to leave AMA and have a treatment failure. You need some successes in your life, and we're willing to work with you to help you. Let me have you answer in two hours."

Sam opted for Plan B. He visited his family, stayed on Antabuse, and attended structured outpatient meetings for four weeks after his return (two weeks longer than if he had stayed in inpatient treatment). He was mainstreamed into aftercare and is still working his program. He learned how to make decisions, how to compromise and how to negotiate with authority figures. He learned how to make a commitment.

It would have been easier for all, the treatment team and Sam, if we had taken the hard-line approach. We could have said, "It's your choice, Sam. Leave if you want to." And Sam would have walked away believing we really didn't care.

We could have made excuses like "He wasn't ready for recovery," or "He was still in denial," or "He's just a sociopath," or "He hasn't hit bottom yet." Instead, we went the extra mile, following the simple rule: Don't allow yourself to assume an adversarial role with crack addicts. Give them a sense of control through well-thought-out options for recovery.

Responding to the Addict's Impulsiveness

Crack addicts are impulsive; they do everything fast. They become addicted fast. They become dysfunctional fast. They come into treatment fast and they think they're recovered . . . fast. They use a hyperdrive drug and tend to adopt a hyperdrive mentality: "If it takes more than ten seconds, how good can it be?"

Counselors can learn to work better with crack addicts by adopting some strategies of counselors who work with another impulsive population, adolescent drug abusers. Across the country today there are many effective chemical dependency programs for adolescents. By studying the techniques used in these programs, we have identified several strategies that are also effective with crack addicts.

Providing Structure. First, provide solid structure in the treatment program, not rigidity, but structure. The treatment program must have firm outer limits, with flexible, adaptable policies and procedures within these limits. The program needs about a half dozen hard-line cardinal rules. Beyond these, there should be policies and procedures for dealing with minor problems that surface during treatment. Both staff and clients need copies of the program's policies and procedures and these should be reviewed in a well-structured, well-delivered orientation to treatment.

Rule and policy violations will occur in a treatment setting. When there is a minor violation of a policy by a client, professionals are better off having written, publicized contingencies already laid out. They may take the form of a menu of possible consequences that the staff and the rule-breaker can select from.

For example, if a crack addict walks out of group, the built-in (and publicized) consequence might be selected from among the following alternatives: (1) write a one-page paper on five past impulsive events that caused later grief; (2) apologize to the group for walking out; (3) spend five minutes on a time-out chair; or, (4) write a one-page paper on how it felt to walk out of group, and then read it to the group next session. By having contingencies in place, the staff is freed from having to come up with reasonable options each time. Clients have a sense of control, knowing there is a menu of consequences.

Making Consequences Known. The consequences of any rule or policy violation should be swift and just. Notice that these are consequences, not punishments. The contingency for the maladaptive behaviors should be therapeutically sound and benefit, not demean, the client. For minor infractions, using a menu system insures quick response to nonadherence issues. For major rule violations, *possible* consequences should be written and publicized to all clients and staff, but the *specific* consequences for an individual client should be handled by the staff alone.

For example, using drugs while in treatment is a major, but common, rule violation. Clients are informed during orientation that using drugs can result in immediate discharge from treatment with the notation, "treatment unsuccessful." While this is a *possible* consequence, it is not the only response that might be selected. The staff should discuss the client's progress to date, the current clinical picture, and any aggravating or mitigating circumstances. Then, the staff should select an appropriate intervention, which may include termination of services or another contingency.

Respond as a Team. Decisions about a major rule violation that could result in service termination should be made in a staff meeting, not by one staff member alone. Having several professional counselors consider appropriate consequences provides a safeguard. Counselors have bad days too, and requiring staff input on major rule violations reduces the chances that an impulsive, and perhaps adverse, decision might be made. Team decisions regarding major rule violations serve as a system of checks and balances.

It is vital to reach a decision on what to do about major rule violations shortly after the event occurs. Crack addicts are impulsive. If you tell them to wait a week to learn the disposition of a rule violation, they may think nothing will ever happen. A week feels like an eternity. Crack addicts are accustomed to being able to change the way they feel in seven seconds, by hitting the pipe. They simply won't wait around feeling anxious and apprehensive for a whole week just to find out the consequences of some behavior. "Nobody waits a week for anything, and certainly not me. I am a crack addict. If I can't have something happen in five seconds, I'm outta here!"

To respond to this without feeding their impulsivity, hold team meetings twice each week to discuss consequences and contingencies for nonadherence to rules. On Mondays the team could deal with problems, or challenges, that surface over the weekend. Thursdays could be used for resolving problems leftover during the week. Thursday is better than Friday for the week's second team meeting, because staff and clients have at least one day to process staff decisions before the weekend.

Reducing AMA Rates

Leaving treatment AMA is related to the crack addict's impulsivity. There are also tactics for minimizing this. First, have a written policies-and-procedures manual for each client. Crack addicts know how to live on the street. They know its rules and regs, its policies and procedures, its dos and don'ts. Because of what they know, crack addicts see the streets as somewhat predictable and, therefore, controllable.

Crack addicts enter treatment with no idea of what to expect. It is a new, strange, and unpredictable experience. Ease the crack addict's mind, lower the anxiety level, and offer a sense of control by teaching what is expected in treatment. A policy-and-procedures manual is a security blanket. When crack addicts receive the manual, they probably will try to memorize its every line so they can better control their fate, to empower themselves. They may become legalistic or twist the rules to prove they are being mistreated, but in doing so they are trying to learn what is normal behavior. This is good because it is one way a crack addicted client gains a sense of control, a human need not unique to crack addicts.

Establish Self-Termination Procedures. Another way to minimize the high AMA rate of crack addicts is to have a written procedure for clients who want to terminate treatment. All programs have admission criteria and "successful" and "unsuccessful" discharge criteria. Yet few programs have a written, publicized policy showing clients the steps they can take to terminate treatment, although it is inevitable that some will choose to do so.

When the staff initiates a policy and procedure for self-termination of treatment, two things happen. First, it normalizes that people are going to feel like walking out of treatment at some time during their recovery. For example, a counselor might say,

"Sometime during the next few weeks, you may want to terminate your treatment. This is normal for a person involved in recovery. When you have those feelings, realize that it's normal. Instead or reacting to those feelings, realize they show the progress you have made. You're starting to think again, getting your mind clear and looking ahead to future goals. Hang in there: the feelings will pass!

"For a few, the feelings will last longer. You may want to discuss them with your counselor or with your peers. Most of your peers have gone through this phase at some point in treatment. They can help you get through it.

"Some of you, very few, will decide to self-terminate your treatment. When clients do this, it's hard on them, hard on their peers in treatment and hard on the staff. We ask anyone who decides to self-terminate to follow standard procedures.

1. Meet with your individual counselor and explain your intention to self-terminate. Spend at least thirty minutes discussing it with your primary counselor.

2. Meet with one other counselor you choose, and discuss your plans to self-terminate. Select a counselor with whom you feel comfortable. Spend about thirty minutes with the second counselor.

3. Let your peers know about your intention to self-terminate. We recommend that you do this in group. You may still choose to leave treatment, but you have a responsibility to let your fellow clients know your reasons. After all, they have been part of your treatment, and you have been part of theirs.

4. Finally, meet with the clinical director. We value your input on our services. We want to be sure that we offer a treatment program that helps clients. If you give us feedback on your treatment experience, it may help others who want to stop their drug problem and improve their lives.

"We hope you'll stick to the commitment you made when you first entered treatment. If we can do anything to help you stick it out, please feel free to talk it over with your counselor or any of our clinical staff. Thank you."

This procedure lets clients know that it is normal and predictable to experience a desire to terminate treatment, and that it should not frighten them. Further, with a written procedure for self-termination of treatment, the AMA rate drops dramatically!

Maintain Client Motivation. There are other ways to minimize the crack addict's high AMA rate. Schedule individual counseling sessions of shorter duration and higher frequency than for other addicts. Instead of sixty-minute counseling sessions scheduled once a week, you can get better results and better client retention with twenty-minute sessions or thirty-minute sessions, two to three times per week. In each session, assign homework that is simple, quick and doable. Make sure the homework requires the crack addict to produce something: write a paper, draw a picture, bring in an object or make a list. Crack addicts need tangible, observable things. The counselor can then post these tangibles, validations of their actual work, on a bulletin board, on a wall or in a notebook with the client's name on it. Clients need to see some tangible results of their efforts or they won't maintain them. The simple act of having a crack addict produce something concrete and post it so that other clients can see it can greatly increase the program's retention rate.

Another productive way of maintaining motivation and involvement is to use workbooks. Workbooks designed for almost any recovery topic are available. They address: the Twelve Steps, decision making, values clarification, relapse prevention, and communication skills, to mention a few. Consider buying some of these. A program staff may also write some exercises and develop workbooks. This is a great way to get the entire treatment team to buy into the program's mission.

Workbooks can be used in individual sessions, family therapy sessions, psychoeducational sessions and in group sessions. Workbook exercises are particularly useful in large group situations. Have the large group work on them together, and post their completed work on flip chart paper. The large group breaks into diads, triads and small groups and each does the project and posts it on flip paper. Before long, the walls of the group room are covered with dozens of sheets of multicolored paper. Use different colored markers so each project has some uniqueness. This provides a validation of work accomplished, productivity and progress. Each addict can look around the room and think, "Wow, I'm really doing something productive here, not simply sitting around talking about doing something."

Criteria-Based Treatment. Another way of increasing crack addicts' retention rate in treatment and to minimize the typically high AMA rate is to divide the treatment environment into a series of short, behaviorally oriented, criteria-based treatment stages. This empowers addicts with a sense of control over the speed in which they advance through therapy and gives them a tangible validation of accomplishments. Consider, for example, the orientation phase, something necessary for all addicts entering treatment. Instead of having a seven-day standard orientation, have an orientation phase varying from three to seven days, depending on client performance. Require clients to accomplish a half-dozen behavioral objectives during the orientation phase. If they accomplish them in three days, they move on to the next phase. If it takes them seven days, that's when they move to the next phase. This empowers them with a sense of control over their treatment. Again, by giving the crack addict options and flexibility within a structured system, the therapist does not have to be in an adversarial role with crack addicts.

Requests For Medication

When crack addicts enter treatment, they may ask frequently for medications. Yes, crack addicts do want drugs. That is all that they have left. They are not unmotivated, just afraid of letting go. Imagine sailing across the Atlantic. The ship sinks! There you are, in the middle of the ocean, treading water. Along floats a barrel of toxic waste. You grab it. But what's that on the horizon? An expert from the Environmental Protection Agency. He shouts, "Hey, buddy, let go of that barrel . . . it will hurt you!" This is similar to the crack addict's dilemma.

Some drugs may be necessary. The counseling profession realizes today that some clients may need medication for the short haul, while others may need certain medications for longer periods. Years of experience and research show that there can be benefits to medications, both pharmatherapeutically and psychotherapeutically. For example, during the initial detox, or stabilization, phase of treatment, there may exist a need for sleeping pills and even benzos. Typically, this need is very short-term for crack addicts.

What about over-the-counter (OTC) medications, such as vitamins and aspirin? Many in the chemical dependency field believe that these pills should be restricted, because to allow them is to condone pill-taking behavior. I would like to remind counselors that the number one predictor of treatment success for crack addicts is the length of time they work an ongoing recovery program. The longer clients are hooked into a therapeutic process (inpatient, out-patient, CA, AA), the higher the probability of long-term success. I see no major problem in giving a crack addict a daily amino acid precursor, or an aspirin, if it will keep that person from leaving treatment AMA. Do we want clients to be perfect, actualized with cosmic consciousness when they leave treatment, or do we want them to be functional? Giving an aspirin to an addict may be enabling the addict, but it definitely removes an excuse for leaving treatment prematurely.

At some time during treatment, the issue of medications must be discussed. Undoubtedly, the crack addict needs to learn not to be so reliant on external substances to fine-tune his daily functioning. Counselors, in their turn, need to put medication issues in proper perspective. There are more critical questions in the first few weeks of treatment than whether the crack addict really needs to take an aspirin today.

Some professionals disagree, feeling that giving the crack addict any medication, at any time, is enabling. Programs dominated by stronger beliefs about controlling all medication use must develop policies with options and contingencies. For example, a policy might permit some OTCs like aspirin, but allow clients no visitors unless they are squeaky clean (no OTCs or other nonprescribed medications) for at least seven consecutive days. This policy inhibits pill taking by clients who want visitors. A policy stating that using OTC medications regularly (for example: three times within seven days), will result in twenty-four-hour bed rest—with no smoke breaks, no socializing, no reading, talking, watching TV or listening to the radio—will slow down pill popping dramatically. Staff who work in an outpatient modality have no control over this issue other than education.

Extraordinary Service Requirements

Treatment professionals have observed that crack addicts demand more services than our other clients; that programs can't keep up with their needs. This is a serious problem. Crack addicts definitely require a wider array of services than well-socialized, employed, married, mainstreamed middle-class alcoholics. Crack addicts usually have more to deal with than compulsive self-administration of a psychoactive substance. Crack addicts have vocational, educational, developmental, sexual, criminal, domestic, childrearing, health and subcultural issues. Their counselors serve as more than chemical dependency counselors. They are employment counselors, vocational counselors, quasi-attorneys, quasi-probation officers, early childhood educators, sex therapists, marriage counselors, parent effectiveness training instructors, quasinurses and health educators, and cultural anthropologists and sociologists. These jobs must be done for too many clients in too little time due to an overtaxed chemical dependency treatment delivery system.

Each counselor may have a caseload of thirty out-patient crack addicts or ten inpatient crack addicts. Many of these clients have pending court appearances for charges ranging from issuing a forged instrument to breaking and entering to sale and possession of crack. Half the caseload is female. Most of these have children younger than five, with no stable family system for childrearing. Some are snow babies, with medical problems, but no medical insurance. Most clients have had some serious sexual traumas, and many have had a sexually transmitted disease. One-third of them currently test positive for some venereal disease. A few have tested HIV positive. Only one-third of them have been employed in the past six months. Only one-half are high school graduates.

No conventionally trained chemical dependency counselor, working alone, can develop a sober or balanced lifestyle for crack addicts. Working with the crack addict requires that chemical dependency professionals either learn case management (i.e. traditional social work) skills or gain the support of a good social worker who can work the bureaucracy. It is far easier to hire a social worker to coordinate legal, educational, medical, vocational, family and child-rearing services than to attempt to teach each counselor the necessary skills for this job. Also, outside social service agencies will respond better to working with one or two social workers than to working with a treatment program's entire clinical staff. When working with crack addicts, get a social worker for case management and collateral liaison with community based, social service agencies.

170

Relapse Prevention

Crack addicts often self-destruct (relapse) immediately after treatment discharge. When the crack epidemic first hit, about 1985, counselors developed aftercare and continuing-care systems based on the population they had the most experience with, the classic alcoholic. Those systems were adapted for crack addicts. They focused on three aspects of recovery: mainstreaming into Twelve-Step fellowship programs, mainstreaming into formal aftercare groups and discharging inpatient or outpatient clients into an environment that was not crack saturated. The Twelve-Step fellowship was the backbone of the recovery program, as well it should be. Crack addicted clients were told to get sponsors, to develop plans for the first ninety days and to come up with names, locations, and times of meetings they would attend. They went to meetings.

Involvement in Self-Help Groups. Crack addicts often found themselves looking for Cocaine Anonymous meetings, first. Unfortunately, there were few CA meetings available. Those available were unstable with little cohesion, with far less sober time among the core group members than is true for Alcoholic Anonymous. Clients often decided to go to AA instead. It was a good idea when one considers that AA had a strong core group of long-standing members with many years of clean time. So, off they went, newly discharged crack addicts, to Alcoholics Anonymous meetings.

One of three things would usually happen at AA. They walked in the door, said, "Hi, I'm George. I'm a crack addict." The entire group would welcome them with open arms. Or the addicts would walk in the door and feel totally out of place around a core group of alcoholics who often had unbelievable amounts of clean time. Crack addicts could not relate to them. Maybe the entire AA meeting would be white, middle-class males, with a few white, middle-class females. Newly discharged crack addicts felt totally out of place and quit going. Or, in the third scenario, crack addicts walked into the AA meeting saying, "Hi, I'm George. I'm a crack addict," to which the AA group responded, "This is AA, you know, for alcoholics!"

We know this really used to happen. It was unfortunate, but true. The good news is that things have changed over the past six years. Now, solid CA meetings are developing in many communities. More AA meetings consist of mixed groups of addicts. Alcoholics welcome crack addicts into the Twelve-Step Fellowship with open arms. AA and CA meetings include racially diverse men and women. The obstacles to finding good Twelve-Step meetings for crack addicts are slowly and progressively disappearing.

Placement in a Stable Environment

The final challenge is the placement of the discharged crack addict into a stable, crack-free environment. Historically, this problem was approached by convincing clients they needed to move from their pretreatment home to a new location, without daily exposure to crack. Many clients listened and moved to a different part of town. They did not have crack cocaine around them, but they didn't have any friends or family either. They did what any normal, healthy, lonely, unsupported person would do. They moved back to the crack-saturated neighborhood. They naturally relapsed.

Today, counselors are responding to this problem by resurrecting the community based storefront program in areas highly saturated by crack cocaine. Programs go into projects where crack is at epidemic levels, open peer counseling and offer drop-in rap group meetings on site. Circuit-riding outreach counselors go into neighborhoods and provide grassroots crisis counseling, relapse prevention counseling and community based social work and case management to clients where they live. We now recognize that moving people away from their homes is not the way to keep them clean and sober. Now counselors identify and build on existing strengths, a realistic, cost-effective, change.

Staff Considerations

Clear policies and good staff supervision are the best way to address the issue of program quality. The following are some key recommendations that can boost the quality and outcomes of chemical dependency treatment programs.

1. Ensure that your program has a clear program philosophy of treatment. To check this out, ask each of the staff at your program what they think the program philosophy is. Hopefully, the responses from all the staff will be consistent. If not, the

program director needs to clearly state it, from the top, and follow up to ensure that the philosophy is heard and understood.

2. Work from the belief that the professionals are at least partially responsible for the clients' treatment and recovery.

3. Don't assume that all assertive, self-directed, and articulate crack addicts are just grandiose, self-centered or impertinent. Addicts are not the only humans who at times become defensive.

4. Don't assume that counselors are competent because they are recovering. Don't assume counselors are competent because they have degrees. Counseling skill is not always directly correlated with life experience or education.

5. If the clients within your program are acting out continuously despite good clinical interventions, change the focus of the interventions toward your staff and not the clients. They may be modeling, or exhibiting systemic parallel process.

6. Ensure that your program has contingency plans for staff who relapse and for staff that become impaired. This is a very challenging and often stressful profession. Have a good Employee Assistance Program, and use it. Explain the services available at the time of hire, and routinely.

AFTERCARE

Meeting Continuing Recovery Needs

For the first few days or weeks following treatment, crack addicts are on a honeymoon with their new love . . . sobriety. But a day comes when they wake up and their lover doesn't look so good. They may want to walk up to strangers on the street and say, "Hey, guess what, I haven't smoked any rocks in two weeks. Pretty good, huh?" But they realize the response would be, "So what? I never smoked crack, you bum!" The public doesn't understand addiction or appreciate recovery, and so the newly recovering addict needs to spend time with people who truly understand.

Aftercare or continuing-care programs provide this understanding support in a less restrictive environment than primary treatment. Continuity of care and an ongoing support system during the critical posttreatment phase improve the addict's chances of remaining drug free by maintaining involvement with others who are struggling with the same problems. Father Joseph Martin, in the classic film, *Chalk Talk*, addresses the difficulty of treating dependency. He stresses that no one person can successfully treat the alcoholic person without the help, resources, and efforts of others. It is a team effort. I believe this applies especially to the crack addict.

Aftercare may involve one or more of the treatment methods already described: individual counseling, treatment planning, group therapy and psychoeducational skill building. An aftercare group works best when it includes socializing, group education, skill building through psychoeducational seminars, group therapy, networking, and fellowship before the close of each session. Aftercare provides an opportunity for people to meet new recovering addicts, to reunite with old buddies, to learn about recovery, to practice what they have just learned, and to share difficulties encountered in the real world.[1]

The most important psychoeducational topics presented or reviewed in aftercare are: *relapse, reentry into the workplace, developing intimacy after recovery, sexuality, developing lists of community resources, financial planning, child rearing, time management (balancing work, education,*

---

1. Dennis Daley has authored a very good psychoeducational workbook for relapse prevention. See: D.C. Daley. *Relapse Prevention Workbook* (Holmes Beach, FL: Blue Nib Ltd., 1986); D.C. Daley, *Relapse Prevention: Treatment Alternatives and Counseling Aids* (Bradenton, FL: Human Services Institute, 1989). Terence T. Gorski, with CENAPS Corporation, has written a great deal on relapse prevention over the past twenty years. See: *Counseling for Relapse Prevention* (Independence, MO: Herald House, 1982). Another book on this topic is: G. A. Marlatt and J.R. Gordon, *Relapse Prevention* (New York: Guilford Press, 1989).

social activities, spiritual activities, personal time, family time)
and the *recovery process*.

Scheduling

A one-day-per-week exposure to an aftercare group, commonly provided by residential treatment programs, is insufficient for the crack addict. Two, one-and-a-half-hour, continuing care groups per week is ideal. More than two aftercare group sessions per week is usually too demanding for the individual and his family. Besides structured aftercare, many clients are likely to attend Twelve-Step groups such as Alcoholics Anonymous, Narcotics Anonymous, Cocaine Anonymous, or Adult Children Of Alcoholics regularly. And then there are often individual counseling sessions every week or two to help keep the general treatment plan focused.

Attending aftercare groups must be made easy for the client. The location of the program is important. Research shows that the distance from a client's home to the aftercare site affects the likelihood of continuing in the program and the continuity of substance free recovery.[2] The time, place, and duration of scheduled aftercare sessions must be reasonable. In the Bible Belt, for example, Wednesday evening is church night. Aftercare groups are

---

2. Research by Prue, Keane, Cornell and Foy (1979) is cited in W. R. Miller. "Motivation for Treatment: A Review With Special Emphasis on Alcoholism," *Psychological Bulletin* 98, no.2(1985): 84-107.

sometimes scheduled for Wednesday evening, creating conflicts and hurting attendance. I once directed an aftercare program that stressed family involvement. It was scheduled for four consecutive hours, from six until ten o'clock in the evening. This places a burden on the staff, with children running around; a burden on the clients and spouses who had to go to work the next morning; and a burden on the children, with school in the morning. This was poor planning.

Twelve-Step Programs

Counselors have an obligation to use all available services that may benefit their clients. Dr. E.M. Jellinek argued, in *The Disease Concept of Alcoholism*, that while Alcoholics Anonymous had achieved notable successes, it would be wrong to accept it as the only viable treatment for addiction.[3] We know that people who follow Twelve-Step programs tend to do well in recovery. *The Cator Report* suggested that AA attendance was highly correlated with total abstinence.[4] Unfortunately, not everyone will attend Cocaine Anonymous, and many who begin eventually drop out. Therefore, the counselor has an obligation to provide a broad menu of aftercare alternatives from which the

---

3. E. M. Jellinek. *The Disease Concept of Alcoholism* (New Haven: New Haven Hillhouse Press, 1960).

4. For more on the CATOR Report, contact: CATOR, 17 West Exchange Street, St. Paul, MN 55102.

client may choose. Primary treatment programs that rely exclusively on Twelve-Step aftercare need to expand their methods and resources.

On the other hand, even a skeptical counselor cannot deny the success of Cocaine Anonymous, and other Twelve-Step programs, in producing ongoing recovery through fellowship and total abstinence from all drugs, "one day at a time." Cocaine Anonymous and related Twelve-Step programs are the primary in-place recovery programs, worldwide. Counselors should always encourage their crack-addicted clients to explore these programs.

An aftercare plan involving Twelve-Step groups gives crack addicts access to open and closed Twelve-Step meetings, and step studies, within the context of the primary treatment program. A mix of on-site and off-site meetings exposes the client to support groups away from the treatment center and helps provide a transition between treatment and aftercare. This helps clients to disengage from the environment where primary treatment occurred and to join a community-based recovery system.

Responding to Relapse

What is the proper way to handle people who relapse and return to aftercare? With great joy. Counselors should consider it flattering when a client has developed enough trust to return and face them after a slip. Let the story be a learning experience for the other clients in aftercare. Handle it in a way that shows the entire group that it is important to come back for help if a slip occurs. Establish and reinforce that norm. An important goal of aftercare is to help clients learn to be interdependent, and to reach out to others when the going gets tough.

THE COUNSELOR

Bringing Out the Best

Counselors have great power and influence over clients, who both look up to them and test them. It appears to me that counselors are loaded guns; they have a tremendous amount of power and influence over their clients, typically, more than they will admit to themselves. I am not sure why this is true. Sometimes, we, as counselors, seem to hate to admit we have a powerful impact on the lives of our clients. We tend to think of ourselves as just like them, or just another human. I don't think that this is true in the eyes of our clients. We are role models, showing our clients through our words and behaviors how a healthy person is supposed to function. We are the path, maybe the only path, the client has to the dream of a drug-free, functional and fulfilling life, at least in their eyes. We may want to minimize the acknowledgment of this power out of our need to be humble, humanistic or egoless. I believe this is a real danger. If we, as counselors, do not acknowledge what is real, we cannot learn to control the influence or ramifications of empowered self. Knowledge sets us free. If we can admit to ourselves that we are loaded guns we can better control when the safety is on or off, and prevent accidental shootings.

Self-Disclose

The counselor's disclosure of a personal history of addiction must be for the client's benefit, not for the counselor's relief from anxiety. Self-disclosure is usually more destructive than no disclosure at all. Chemical dependency counselors often resort to self-disclosure in reaction to a situation instead of as a way to act on a situation, as part of a carefully constructed plan. Whenever counselors react to crack addicts in therapy without a well thought out plan, they run the risk of disaster. If you self-disclose, do it consciously, not reactively. For best results, do so at a process level, not at a content level.

For example, take a situation where a client claims no one can understand him because he was raised in a violent family. As a result, he spent half his life in prison. A content self-disclosure response might be: "I understand. I went to prison for three years for robbery, because I was raised in a lousy family, too" or, "I can relate. I spent six months in a road camp for beating a guy in a bar." A process self-disclosure response would be: "I understand you feel like no one has walked in your shoes, that no one can understand. Well, I've had some tough times in my life too, times when I felt hopeless, isolated and cursed by my past. But you know what? There was reason for hope."

When clients walk out of your office after a content self-disclosure, they remember that you are a crook and a thug, not that you can relate to them. If anything, you will have convinced the client that you are more screwed up than he is, so why go to you for help?

I have often witnessed chemical dependency counselors self-disclose specific contents of their pasts. It invariably returns to haunt or discredit them. I have made that mistake too. Rarely, if ever, does self-disclosure *at a process level* backfire though.

Self-disclosure should always be made for the benefit of the client, and not to relieve the anxiety of the counselor. In many ways, the counseling profession uses self-disclosure the same way they use confrontation. It's a professionally acceptable way to unload, on a client, issues that we can't sort out ourselves. Instead of using self-disclosure as a bail-out mechanism when stuck in tough clinical situations, take a five-minute break from the session to cool down. It is vital that counselors know and practice this strategy. Both therapists and clients will appreciate the relief.

Avoiding the "I've Been There Too" Mistake

Regression is a defense mechanism against excessive anxiety, low self-concept, and self-depreciation. When under pressure, most people regress to a more solid, familiar way of functioning. They look for a method of functioning they know best, preserving a sense of inner comfort. Recovering addicts, who work as chemical dependency counselors, need to be careful not to regress to the "I'm a dope fiend (or drunk) too!" role when under pressure. It happens in situations like this:

A counselor is conducting a group or individual session that is out of control. The clients confront him aggressively and challenge the professional's ability to do the job. Complaints fly: "You don't understand where we're coming from." "Why do we have to learn this stuff? What does this have to do with drugging?" If the counselor senses that he has gotten into a situation exceeding the limits of his own professional competence, he may revert to the client role, saying, "Hey, I've been there too. I am one of you. I used to shoot more dope than you have ever seen. I used to drink more booze in one day than you have in your lifetime."

The counselor's regression to a client role benefits neither the crack addict nor the counselor. Crack addicts need stable, healthy role models, not another dysfunctional addict to counsel them. Imagine how clients must feel during episodes like the one described above. They enter treatment because they were out of control and need guidance and direction. Yet in the above scenario, the counselor appears equally out of control. The counselor's job is to be a resource person, a guide. If the crack-addicted client wanted advice from an addict, he would have sought it on the street, where advice is cheap. The chances are that he has already done this, unsuccessfully, and there now remains no firm belief that another addict has the answers. The professional therapist needs to continue to be the professional counselor, not just an addict who works with other addicts.

Counselor or True Believer?

Just because a program saved your life doesn't mean it owns your mind. Many chemical dependency counselors credit a certain treatment program with saving their lives. They consider this program and its staff, as almost sacred. Those folks, in that specific program, were the first people we ever trusted. They are the first people who trusted us even though we were addicts, the first people to see us cry, to see us feel weak and still respect us. That program opened our eyes to a better life, a life with dignity, respect for ourselves, and a life that would allow the giving and receiving of love. We have a lot to be grateful for, but we need to set limits on how we show that gratitude.

An unwritten law states that clients should have at least two years of recovery before being considered for a staff position. Research tells us the newly recovering addict (less than one year in recovery) often lacks the empathy and emotional detachment necessary to work effectively with other addicts. During the first year of recovery addicts learn to live with themselves. During the second year, they learn to live with other human beings. Then they are ready to work in chemical dependency treatment. Simply abstaining for two years posttreatment doesn't prove anyone's motivation or appropriateness for a staff position with a chemical dependency treatment program. It is wise to require that the aspiring counselor have some documentation of career planning toward the helping profession during that two-year period of sobriety. This may be volunteer work with a social service agency. It may be college work in counseling or social services. It is wise to look for both. Programs should be staffed with competent people who feel a sense of mission.

Skill Counts

You are employed as a CD counselor because you have skills, not because you sat in college for four years or once were an addict. There has been infighting between recovering and nonrecovering professionals. Recovering counselors often have life experiences that substitute for formal education. The nonrecovering are typically overrepresented by people with college degrees. Therefore, the fight is now commonly seen as a match between the "book-taught counselor who does not know anything about the real world," and, in the other corner, the "just an old drunk who does not understand human behavior." This must stop.

So how does a counselor relate honestly with clients while still maintaining professional respect? My response to questions about myself and recovery is, "I won't tell you. I am here to present information that will help you improve your skills. If I say I am recovering, some of you will join with me immediately. You'll listen attentively and probably stereotype me. You'll think you know what I believe, feel and think. Others will simply say that I am just an old dope fiend with no real worth. If I say I am nonrecovering, some of you will join with me immediately, listen attentively and probably stereotype what I believe, feel and think. Others will simply say that I'm just an old college type with no real worth. My goal is to convey information and to have you hear it. I don't want your biases to filter out my information."

A recovering counselor can be a more effective counselor than one who is nonrecovering under certain circumstances. Two counselors are equal in every way: educationally, intellectually, interpersonally, intrapersonally, with exact levels of internal motivation, creativity, diligence, dedication, commitment, persuasion skills, compassion, firmness, flexibility, understanding, knowledge, strength, wisdom, ethics, spontaneity and self-awareness, but one is recovering and the other not. The best bet would be to hire the recovering person. Yet, how often are two people that similar? The wise decision would be to use these other virtues and skills as a criteria for measuring better instead of the experience of having consumed or not consumed psychoactive substances in a compulsive, out-of-control manner.

The best staffing pattern for a treatment program blends fifty percent recovering with fifty percent nonrecovering counselors. The recovering counselors should have attained sobriety in different ways, not through just one specific method. That helps insure that a program won't develop a narrow, doctrinaire approach to treatment, recovery, and relapse prevention.

Credentials. Every counselor who works in the chemical dependency field needs to be credentialed in that field.

An M.D. needs a specialization in addictions treatment. A mental health counselor needs a C.A.C. A recovering person needs a Certified Addictions Professional certificate on the office wall.

When a counselor is validated as a professional by an outside organization such as a state or national licensing board, a certification board, or a professional organization's credentialing board, the recognition helps create a feeling of pride. Credentials help during those times when the counseling is not going right; when clients do not change their behaviors, when we feel inadequate or inept in our jobs. At those times we can look at the credentials on the wall to remind us of our skills and commitment.

Credentials ease the concerns of clients. Imagine walking into a physician's office and seeing nothing on the wall, no degrees. Attorney's offices without college degrees, awards, certificates or credentials seem pretty frightening. On the other hand, seeing a medical degree from Harvard, postdoctoral training at Johns Hopkins and certification from the Board of Surgeons makes a patient feel a little more confident and secure. The patient tends to trust the doctor a little more. The same is true for counselors. Walk into your office and ask yourself how you would feel if you came into that office seeking help for a problem.

Certification gives the counselor something of value that can be removed if one fails to maintain professionalism. One violation of the licensing/credentialing organization's code of professional ethics takes away that piece of paper. This knowledge can influence every professional's ethical behavior.

Besides appropriate credentials, counselors need good supervision. Important decisions should be based on inter-disciplinary team concepts, using the mechanisms that exist to intervene with staff should they lose sight of appropriate ethics. We cannot tolerate unethical behaviors. Our clients are too fragile.

Chemical dependency counselors serve as role models for clients, representing the treatment staff, the program, and the profession. Even when they aren't aware of it, counselors can function as role models. Here is an ex-ample from my experience:

Tom (not his real name) entered treatment into a therapeutic community I was directing. The program was a behavior modification based modality. The average stay was from six to ten months.

It was obvious at the time of admission into treatment that Tom didn't trust this treatment stuff, but, like many new clients, his spirit had been broken by the drug-using lifestyle. He needed a break from it. Tom had a strange habit. Each morning when I arrived at the program and entered the building, there he was, looking me dead in the eyes. He wouldn't say a word, just stare into my eyes. Very peculiar, I thought. This behavior continued each morning, Monday through Friday, for nearly six consecutive months.

Tom graduated from our program. He returned to school, completed his GED and began courses with the local junior college. He volunteered with several social service agencies. He coled group counseling sessions with methadone program clients and volunteered with the local crisis line agency. After two years of sobriety, he began working with me in a short-term program I directed. Then, as a co-worker, I finally asked Tom to explain why he had watched and stared at me every day.

Tom explained, "George, every day you came to work and you were happy. You were optimistic. You joked with the staff and clients. You seemed to love your job. I knew you must be high to always be so happy. I wanted to catch you high. I wanted to be able to discount everything I was learning in treatment by catching you high just once. Then I could tell myself that this treatment stuff was just another con job. I could believe there really wasn't such a thing as a life where people like themselves, like others and like what they are doing. After six months of watching you and not catching you high, I realized it was possible to be happy and not high. Thank you."

You, as a counselor, are a role model, and at times, a limit setter. I think this is especially true when working with crack addicts who often, maybe even typically, have great developmental deficits and never have had the opportunity to be adequately parented or socialized. You are the standard by which they measure normalcy. The addict will bounce pathology off you to see if and how the standard of normalcy will act or react to the pathology. The addict will test limits to see where those limits end, and if they are flexible and consistent. You as a therapist must be willing to set those limits, avoid negative contracts or negative coalitions, and often, as a parent must do, say no even though it hurts you inside. You are there for the benefit of the client. Your actions need to be governed by what will contribute to the overall good of the client, not the comfort level of yourself. Further, I think it is important to keep in mind that you don't need to take this limit testing and pathology bouncing personally. It is normal, predictable, and essential if the addict is to learn mature functioning.

CONCLUSION

The field of chemical dependency treatment has undergone major changes during the past ten years, especially since the onset of the crack epidemic of 1985. Counselors have found themselves to be a profession with a model of addiction treatment that may not fit the population they are now treating.

Years ago, counselors conceptualized addiction as a linear continuum of impairment, going from use to abuse to addiction. They created good strategies for treating the addicted, and did not really focus exclusively on the defects and deficits of the user or the abuser. With the dramatic increase in illicit drug use in America and court referrals into treatment, counselors now encounter many clients before they reach the final stage in this continuum. Users and abusers, as well as addicts, enter into our treatment programs. However, the system was developed for alcohol addicts in the latter stage of their addiction. The cookie cutter does not seem big enough to encompass the full continuum of impairments reflected in our caseloads, especially crack addicts.

Treatment programs have attempted to deal with this, not by expanding the cookie cutter to include users and abusers, but by trying to classify all clients as if they are latter-stage alcohol addicts, using standard treatment methods developed for this group. This has not worked well. Now the field faces a need to develop alternative strategies to work with diverse types of addicts and to go beyond the generic treatment methods used with classic gamma alcoholics. It is time to face the challenge of treating the crack addict . . . the person, not the addiction.

I hope this book has helped reach this goal by giving you some new and useful ideas about treating the crack cocaine addict. I have taken eighteen years of clinical experience, ten years of college education, and forty-one years of life and frozen them, my thoughts, feelings and beliefs about addiction and treating the crack addict, onto paper. In looking back at what I have written, there are several key ideas that should be reemphasized in closing.

- A client's total abstinence from drugs does not necessarily mean that the chemical dependency treatment has been successful. Successful recovery involves adequate functioning in daily life. Abstinence is a precursor to functionality, not a substitute for it.

- Empower your clients. The goal of treatment is to do everything possible to build up the person's self-image and self-concept, not to make them passive, acquiescent drones. Build 'em up!

- Don't impose a treatment on the client. Offer a choice of options. This gives the client a sense of control, even while under direction.

- Stroke your clients more. Counselors do not always show enough appreciation for clients who are doing well in their program.

- It is easier to turn a "no" into a "yes" than to turn a "yes" into a "no." When pushed to make a decision, you can always decide to wait. When forced to make a decision before you feel the time is right, start with "no."

- Practice and believe in empathy. It is still the leading factor in productive therapeutic relationships.

I hope this book has validated what you are now doing as a counselor, and if not, that it has challenged you to reconsider some important treatment issues. Together, our knowledge will grow, and we will learn more science and magic as we continue our struggle and commitment to discover the most effective ways of treating cocaine addiction. Counseling the crack addict takes practice, dedication and patience. It takes skill. It means getting your hands messy. It is a tough job that demands special kinds of people.

Carl Rogers speaks of empathy, the ability to feel what a person feels as if you are going through it yourself, without ever forgetting the "as if." Empathy is going heart-to-heart with another human, and having the courage and respect to join in the emotional roller coaster while maintaining our belief in the goodness and dignity of humans; a philosophy of life that will, through our relationship with it, allow us personal healing when we find the tragedies around us creeping into our own hearts.

INDEX